Management and the
Social Sciences

AN ADMINISTRATIVE STAFF COLLEGE PUBLICATION

Other Administrative Staff College Publications

On Thinking Statistically: M. B. Brodie
Biography in Management Studies: Humphrey Lloyd
Writers on Organizations: D. S. Pugh, D. J. Hickson & C. R. Hinings
New Thinking in Management: F. de P. Hanika

Tom Lupton

Montague Burton Professor of Industrial Relations,
University of Leeds

Management and the
Social Sciences

AN ESSAY

HUTCHINSON OF LONDON

HUTCHINSON & CO (*Publishers*) LTD
178–202 Great Portland Street, London w.1

London   Melbourne   Sydney
Auckland   Bombay   Toronto
Johannesburg   New York

First published 1966

*This book has been set in Bembo type face. It has been printed in Great Britain by
Benham and Company Limited, Colchester,
and bound by Wm. Brendon and Son Ltd, Tiptree, Essex*

Acknowledgements

Morris Brodie and Andrew Life of the Administrative Staff College suggested many improvements of style and presentation which I have incorporated. Their constructive criticisms also led to changes in the content of Part IV. I am grateful to them.

More generally, I have to thank the many practising managers I have met while researching in industry and during my teaching career. Their questions about, and criticisms of, social science have helped form the views I have expressed here.

My debt to my academic colleagues, whose work I have briefly and I hope accurately cited, will be obvious.

I am also grateful to the following for permission to quote extracts: the University of Chicago Press for the quotation from a paper by Chester Barnard in the *Journal of Business*; Harvard University Press for the quotations from *Management and the Worker* by Professor F. J. Roethlisberger and W. J. Dickson; Her Majesty's Stationery Office and Miss Joan Woodward for the extract from *Management and Technology*; Oliver & Boyd Ltd. and Professor Max Gluckman for a quotation from *Closed Systems and Open Minds*; Prentice-Hall Inc., Dean Cyert and Professor March for comments on the economists' theory of the firm taken from *A Behavioral Theory of the Firm*; Tavistock Publications (1959) Ltd. and A. K. Rice for a note on a conceptual framework elaborated in *The Enterprise and its Environment*.

TOM LUPTON

Leeds University

v

I believe a good deal of conflicting bunk is taught in these fields. This argues for improvement and development, not against teaching what can be taught. In the time of Newton, or even much later, a great deal of modern physics, and much that is fundamental in it, was not known, and for this reason perhaps a good deal of bunk was then taught in that field.

Education for Executives CHESTER BARNARD[1]

Contents

Author's Note

This essay has two main objectives: firstly to introduce the social science of organizations to those managers who have no previous knowledge of it, secondly to dispel such scepticism as to its practical value as may exist amongst those who have already encountered the methods and findings of social science.

Part I discusses the various social sciences and their subject matter and goes on to describe some early theories about industrial organization as developed by social scientists and managers.

Part II summarizes some researches carried out by social scientists in industry. These illustrate the methods and the research procedures of social science—particularly sociology—and the knowledge about industrial organizations as social systems which is accumulating.

Part III considers more specifically what social science has to offer to the manager by referring to some practical problems, e.g. of industrial conflict and co-operation, of communication, and of technical change.

Part IV, finally, is a short section outlining some current developments in the theory of organizations.

I

Early Contributions to Theory

Early Contributions to Theory

Social science certainly includes Sociology, Social Anthropology, Social Psychology and Political Science. Some other branches of psychology and also economics might well be included. If I were asked for a brief personal definition of social science I would include all activities which are concerned systematically to investigate and to explain aspects of the relation between the individual and the society of which he is a part. All the fields of study mentioned rest on a belief that there are regularities in social life which may be observed and which have causes which may be discovered, just as there are regularities in the physical world which are the concern of the so-called physical sciences. Each Social Science chooses to abstract from the complex processes of social life different relations between events, and to approach the study of them using different methods. Max Gluckman, a distinguished social anthropologist, has recently put it like this:

'. . . the different social and behavioural sciences are in the main distinguished not by the events they study, but by the kind of relation between events that they seek to establish. Events themselves are neutral to the different disciplines.'[2]

What, then, do the different social sciences study? Economists are chiefly interested in the problems of rational choice between economic alternatives in situations of scarcity, uncertainty and risk. Social psychologists study the problems arising for individuals from their membership of small social groups. Sociologists are concerned chiefly with the structuring and interlocking of social roles at work, in the family, the factory, the residential community and other 'bits' of society, and the associated problems of social order. Social Anthropologists look at the same problems—usually, but not always, in non-industrialized societies—and employ somewhat different methods of inquiry and analysis. Political Scientists are interested in questions of power in society, its origins, and how it is legitimated and administered.

There are obvious areas of overlap between the various social sciences but it is easy to see how all of them might come to be interested in industrial organizations. In industry there are problems of maintaining social order which are of interest to the political scientist and the sociologist, problems arising in relationships between social groups which attract the sociologist and the social anthropologist, and problems of the adjustment of the individual to the group which the social psychologist might wish to investigate. Then there is the effect of the physical environment on the health and well-being of the employee. This, and its influence on industrial relationships, is investigated by a branch of psychology known as industrial psychology.

The various social sciences all take as a subject for study one or other aspect of the same complex reality. Reality is, as it were, taken apart for the purpose of study, and the industrial firm is a good place to study many of its aspects. But it would seem that for the manager, or the trade union official—the practical administrator—reality is all of a piece and has to be dealt with as such. Any one of their administrative activities might pose, at one and the same time, problems of rational choice between economic alternatives, problems of inter-group relations, problems of structure, power and authority, and problems of personal idiosyncrasy. In point of fact, managers do not deal with complex reality as a whole. When they try to theorize and to explain behaviour, they do what social scientists do: they break up reality into compartments; and when they act, they act from partial theories—as practical economists, for example, or practical psychologists.

It is because the reality of social life is so complex as to defy the efforts of theorists and practical men fully to understand and explain it, that our knowledge of the behaviour of human beings individually and collectively is of necessity fragmented and in consequence difficult to apply. There are two courses open. Either we give up trying to understand and explain and rely exclusively and riskily on practical personal flair, or we seek better ways to understand and to explain, and to make our understandings and explanations available for practical men to use. This latter activity is, as I see it, the social role of social science.

Not all social scientists are interested in the problems of industrial organization, but during the last seven or eight decades, the emergence of large-scale industrial organizations of increasing complexity has attracted social scientists in greater numbers to the study of their problems. On the whole, the interest of economists in the problems of decision making *within* organizations is recent in origin. The psychologists were first in the field and their concern was then largely with the effect of physical environment. Then came social psychology and sociology. Only very recently have political scientists begun to take an interest. The social anthropologists, especially in the U.S.A., have long worked on industrial problems. As a result of all this work the possiblity now exists of a social science of organization which will draw upon the methods and findings of all the social sciences.

The range of problems all these social scientists have studied and written about is really quite narrow and easy to comprehend. They relate to the difficulties for human individuals and groups which arise from working in organizations and from trying to make organizations work more effectively. Industrial social scientists are interested particularly in:

1. The consequences of various ways of allocating and distributing work and authority, i.e. in problems of structure.
2. The nature of conflict and co-operation in organizations and their relation to structure.
3. Human motivation, satisfaction, and incentives.
4. The communication of ideas, orders, and information.
5. Physical and mental health and its relation to the physical and social environment of the individual.
6. Technical and administrative change.

The rest of this section is devoted to a summary description of the efforts of social scientists and others to throw light on some of these problems and to improve industrial performance as one consequence.

EARLY STUDIES BY TAYLOR AND THE SCIENTIFIC MANAGERS

The intellectual origins of the contemporary social science of industrial organization are many. From the beginning of organized social life man has theorized, speculated and moralized about the relations of the individual in and to society. Yet it would be fair, I believe, to trace the origins of the systematic study of *industrial* organizations to F. W. Taylor[3] and other 'scientific managers' such as Gantt and Gilbreth. These men were not professional philosophers, or social scientists. They were intelligent and energetic practical managers, driven by the problems of their time to a pre-occupation with the relationship between the individual and the organization of the enterprise in which he worked. At the end of the nineteenth century, when Taylor began to practise and to write about his ideas, the problem of achieving efficiency in large, technically complex factories was a relatively new one. He considered that the main obstacle to efficiency was a failure by managers to find ways to co-ordinate and control the work of industrial operatives while at the same time offering rewards for their co-operation which would satisfy them. Specifically, he claimed that managers had not systematically studied the work of operators in order to find better methods of working, but had left that to the operators with disastrous results for efficiency; nor had managers paid sufficient attention to the control of the work of operators by personal supervision and various incentives. He himself set out to devise methods of job study, control of work flow and incentives, and he succeeded brilliantly.

It is not necessary in a book written for managers by a social scientist to describe the technical achievements of scientific management. They are to be seen in time and motion study, systems of payment by results, production control systems, and so on. What is of interest here is the theory about the organization and the individual which is implicit in Taylor's techniques.

Taylor could discern no reason beyond bad management for conflict between the worker on the one hand and the owners and the managers on the other. It was evident to him that the prosperity of the working man was tied to the prosperity of the firm. Therefore, any steps to improve that prosperity, such as by the methods of scientific management, would be welcomed once it was explained that this *was* the objective, and that the individual worker would benefit. He, the worker, would also accept the division of the task in which the managers and the technical specialists were the organizers and the controllers, and the industrial operators the 'doers', because he would see this, as Taylor himself did, as a prerequisite of efficiency. Therefore, the movement to end 'rule-of-thumb management', which was Taylor's life's work, was regarded by him not only as a contribution to industrial efficiency but also as a specific remedy for industrial strife and management–worker conflict in all its forms.

As engineers concerned with a problem of the organization of manual workers, the scientific managers stressed the significance of physical activities. For them, the industrial worker was a kind of mechanism who would, if he were given the right rewards, submit to being 'set-up' to produce, in predetermined ways, certain defined bits of work. This summary, although in its essentials fair, is, however, too crude adequately to represent Taylor's thought. He and the other scientific managers always stressed the importance of getting the 'right atmosphere', of taking account of the attitudes of workers, and of the necessity to explain. But the procedures for getting the 'right' atmosphere never were worked out systematically. The theoretical framework of scientific management, with its crude psychology and sociology, was inadequate for this task.

When Taylor and his colleagues observed behaviour which was not prescribed by the organization as formally necessary to achieve its objectives, their attitude was to condemn rather than to explain. For example, the practice of groups of workers setting 'ceilings' on output, below the targets set by managers, was to Taylor 'an evil'. He regarded 'systematic soldiering', as he called it, as an understandable reaction to a lack of proper control by management, and the working man was therefore not to be individually condemned for it. But it benefited nobody, and it was demoralizing, and so it was 'an evil'. Taylor's ideas of human motivation were primitive, and he never understood the significance of groups in organizations. Organizations were seen as disorderly aggregates of individual human beings drilled into formal order and given direction by formal structure and procedures of planning and control instituted by management.

All these criticisms of scientific management have the benefit of hindsight. Contemporaries of Taylor who criticized his methods, and there were many, mostly did so on the humanitarian ground that 'speed-up' was a bad thing for the health and well-being of workers. There were also trade union critics busy averting a threat to their interests and the interests of their members as they saw them. For Taylor had no use for trade unions and blamed them for encouraging restrictive practices which, as he argued, were *against* the workers' interests. There is, so far as I am aware, no contemporary critique of Taylor based on a charge of theoretical inadequacy. These were to come later.

MAX WEBER AND BUREAUCRACY

Max Weber (1864 to 1920) was a contemporary of Taylor. This German scholar has greatly influenced modern sociology and, like Taylor, though for different reasons, he was interested in formal organization, i.e. in the rational means employed to direct the activities of many individuals with different jobs towards given objectives.

Weber was a student of the history of social organization. He wrote much about the many forms of social organization found in human history and he theorized about the reasons for their emergence and decline. (4) From our point of view it is his interest in modern bureaucracy which matters. In everyday usage bureaucracy is synonymous with red tape and inefficiency. In Weber's usage it is a type of organization. Bureaucracy will rarely be found in its pure form but it is, as it were, a prototype for an efficient modern large-scale organization. Unlike Taylor, Weber was not a passionate advocate for his theories, nor a practical administrator. He was, as a scholar, interested in what was happening in industrialized societies and in trying to find ways systematically to describe it and compare it with what was happening elsewhere and what had happened in other periods of history. From his inquiries have come ideas and ways of thinking about organizations which still influence social scientists.

What intrigued Weber about large-scale modern organizations was the method by which they perpetuated themselves. Individuals came into organizations, worked in them, left them, and the organizations continued to exist. Why? How does an organization exercise authority over the persons who for the time being are its members? In short how is it managed? He distinguished three elements which together constitute what he called bureaucratic authority:
1. Fixed official duties.
2. Rules about authority and coercion.
3. Methodical provision for the fulfilment of duties and the exercise of rights.

To take these in order: bureaucracies are distinguished by the methodical way they distribute and define official duties. That is to say they define certain areas of competence. In industrial parlance, care is taken about job descriptions throughout the organization and the way the jobs interrelate. Now official duties carry responsibilities for getting things done. To get things done necessitates having authority to impose sanctions and to distribute rewards. But this power must be limited by the rules which govern the office. It must not be arbitrary. There is, in a bureaucracy, a special concern to see that persons are competent to fulfil the duties and obligations of the office they occupy. Therefore, selection and training for office, done systematically, must be a feature of bureaucracy. Since bureaucracies have hierarchical, pyramid shaped, social structures, with greater authority and heavier responsibility at the top than at the bottom, they tend to provide for continuity at the top by recruitment from the layers below. The prospect of promotion acts as a spur to organizational loyalty and ensures efficient successors at every level, provided that careful selection and training is devised to that end and proper qualifications specified.

A bureaucracy also ensures permanence by the keeping of files and records, i.e. the 'know how' remains in the organization and does not pass out with individuals who leave. It tends to separate the organizational life of the incumbent of office from his private life and to imbue in him ideas of service to the organization as a profession or vocation.

The nearest thing to Weber's notion of bureaucracy is the civil service, but it is not difficult to see in his description features of large-scale industrial firms and perhaps some small ones. It is not difficult either to see that in a sense Taylor and the scientific managers exemplified the processes of bureaucratization that Weber described. They were certainly interested in defining areas of competence, in distributing authority and in methodical provision for the performance of duties and the exercise of rights. They were mainly interested, however, in the organization of manual work. Discussion of the theory and practice of bureaucratic *management* is to be found in the writings of those whom I have chosen to describe as *the theorists of formal organization*. The work of these writers, particularly Fayol and Urwick, will be described presently.

In Taylor's time psychologists had not yet shown much interest in the problems of the individual in an industrial context, although there were isolated exceptions. The problems of industrial organization in the first world war stimulated the application of psychological knowledge to industry and gave birth to *industrial psychology*.

THE BRITISH INDUSTRIAL PSYCHOLOGISTS

The problem of creating organizations which are efficient and which at the same time satisfy the desires, aspirations and interests of those who work in them has attracted workers from all the social sciences, as well as practical administrators. Max Weber saw the problem largely as one of constructing a rational system of authority for the efficient pursuit of defined objectives. He was therefore concerned more with problems of social structure than with the psychological problems of adjusting persons to roles. He was probably inclined to assume that this could be taken care of by careful role definition, by selection and training and by a rational system of rewards and punishments in the organizations. In many respects Taylor took the same position, although he was greatly concerned with the details of systems of rewards and punishments for industrial workers. Industrial Psychologists placed the emphasis much more on the problems of the individual in carrying out his organizational role than on the design of the organization. One reason for this · was the tradition of the psychology of their time which was interested especially in explaining and measuring the differences between individuals. Another was the type of problems confronting the psychologists.

The first industrial researches of any consequence by psychologists were done in England in the first world war under the auspices of the Health of Munition Workers' Committee and its successor the Industrial Fatigue Research Board. The scarcity of labour, the large influx of women into industry and the insatiable demand for munitions defined the problems to be studied. How many hours a day can a man, or woman, go on working and still come each morning fit for each new day's work? What effect do poor lighting and ventilation have on the level of output of industrial workers? Are there any ways of improving the methods of work so that output improves and at the same time the work is made easier, less boring, more satisfying? These problems demanded that existing knowledge of physical and mental fatigue had to be applied and new knowledge gained. There were also the problems of the proper selection and training of industrial workers to be investigated and new systems to be devised.

So useful was this work that it was carried on after the war.[5] Although a wider range of problems is now studied, the tradition is continued to this day by the Industrial Psychology Unit of the Medical Research Council. The National Institute of Industrial Psychology, a private foundation, established in 1921, does much the same range of research work. Its main support comes from industry and it has a very practical bent. At its inception there was some suspicion that it was practising Taylorism under another name, whereupon it was explained that the work of the N.I.I.P. was based upon sound psychology rather than on a mechanical analogue of the human being. It sought not to push the worker from behind but to ease his difficulties, and by this means to increase his output and his personal satisfaction. In recent years, as psychological knowledge has grown, the N.I.I.P. has increased the range of its research and consulting work, but it is still very much concerned with physical working conditions, selection procedures and the like.

Although the British psychologists were right to say that they were not Taylorists, they were, like Taylor, interested in finding ways to improve the productive performance of industrial workers, while at the same time keeping the workers healthy and satisfied. They differed in that the psychologists had a much more refined conception of the complexities of the individual human organism and were interested in the further refinement of that conception. Like Taylor, they also emphasized the physical rather than the social (organizational) environment, although they showed an awareness of the positive influence of the latter which was lost on Taylor.

The differences and the similarities between Taylor and the early industrial psychologists are illustrated by their approach to the subject of rest pauses for manual workers. Both were interested in so arranging spells of work and rest that output would be maximized. The rapid onset of fatigue after long spells of work was to be avoided by judiciously spaced rest periods. In this way the worker would go home healthily tired at the end of the day having done a good day's work. But Taylor had a crude common-sense theory about fatigue, a lack of appreciation of the influence of sentiment in human working relationships, and homespun ideas of motivation. Nor, for all his commitment to science, did he seem to be aware of a need to improve on common sense in explaining human behaviour. The industrial psychologists were aware of this need and worked with admittedly imperfect but tested knowledge about, for example, human muscular fatigue, human motivation, and human instincts and emotions.

The work of the industrial psychologist in the past fifty years has had its impact on industry. Much is now known and applied about selection procedures, about methods of training, and about fatigue; and the psychologists have contributed greatly to the design of machines and buildings, so that these are more appropriate to the needs of the working human being.

It is not my intention here to attempt to describe in detail the findings of the industrial psychologists, or even to summarize them. But they play an important part in the story of social science and industry.

One of the early homes of industrial psychology was Harvard University. From its Graduate School of Business and from Professor Elton Mayo in particular came the idea of the researches at the

Hawthorne works of the Western Electric Company near Chicago. These experiments, which began in the tradition of British industrial psychology, were to have a marked effect on the development of the application of social science to industry, and on the practice of management.

ELTON MAYO AND THE HAWTHORNE EXPERIMENTS

It is as well to begin a brief account of the Hawthorne experiments with a reminder that the problem being studied was the same general problem as had faced all the other inquirers whose work we have discussed, namely what are the factors in the physical and social environment of the person working in an organization which affect his working performance and his personal satisfaction with his work? Like the British industrial psychologists, the Hawthorne researchers had a strong applied bent—they wanted to use their findings to improve output and satisfaction at the Hawthorne plant, as well as to add to the stock of knowledge in social science.

In November 1924 some experiments on the effect on output of lighting of various intensities were started. These were carried out in actual working departments and the results showed no positive relation between the two variables. It was therefore assumed that the experimental design was faulty and that better isolation and control of the variables should be attempted. A test group and a control group were formed. The surprising result was a similar and appreciable increase of output *in both groups*. The experimenters were puzzled but persistent. Their further efforts, however, only led them inexorably to the conclusion that it was impossible to isolate and measure one or two variables when studying a 'natural' work group. They therefore decided to set up experimental groups in which it would be easier to isolate and measure the variables, and for their first study with such groups they chose the problem of rest pauses and fatigue. These were problems with which, as we saw, the industrial psychologists and Taylor had been greatly concerned. The Hawthorne investigators were sure that their own experiences with the lighting experiments cast doubt on the methods by which existing knowledge of rest pauses and fatigue had been gained; they set out to remedy this by careful experimental design.

But the results of subsequent experiments left the experimenters a little puzzled. After all their carefully controlled changes in hours of work, rest pauses and so on, they were unable to halt a general upward trend in the rate of output. Even a lengthening of the working day and a reduction of rest pauses seemed to have little or no depressing effect. To quote the researchers: 'the general upward trend, despite changes, was astonishing.'[6]

The problem raised set the investigators planning further experiments to test the effects of changes in methods of wage payment on output, or of changes in the supervisor–worker relationship; effects which it was suspected had intervened adventitiously to influence earlier experiments. The experimenters were led a step further to the conclusion that every factor in a work situation is so closely related to all the others that any attempt to hold one constant will change the others.

For example—and I quote the researchers' own words—

'. . . the efficiency of a wage incentive was so dependent on its relation to other factors that it was impossible to consider it as a thing in itself having an independent effect on the individual.'[7]

The management of the factory began to see that:

' . . . such factors as hours of work and wage incentives were not things in themselves having an independent effect upon employees' efficiency; rather, these factors were no more than parts of a total situation and their effects could not be predicted apart from that total situation.'[8]

Now the methods of the investigators changed. They were looking at the organization and its constituent departments as a social system and not as aggregations of individuals who were passive recipients of pushes and pulls in the direction of increased efficiency. But not only did their methods change—the break with tradition was more remarkable in that they began to give importance not to lighting, ventilation, rest pauses, selection and so on but to attitudes, to social relationships at work, and to supervisory behaviour. In short they were moving nearer to a theory which took account of the characteristics of the individual and the way these influenced, and were influenced by, relationships in the organization. The researchers concluded that attention should be directed to the definition of the role of the supervisor and his selection and training, because his behaviour was a major influence on morale. They also recommended a programme of confidential interviews to give workers an opportunity to complain, to suggest or simply to let off steam.

The Hawthorne experiments suggested that interferences with the equilibrium between the individual and the social reality around him were not due, at any rate in the Hawthorne works, to physical conditions, i.e. they did not arise from fatigue, monotony, boredom, etc. Nor were they due to neurosis, i.e. to failures in the mental capacity of individuals to adjust to reality. These interferences arose out of the social relations of the individual both outside the factory and on the job.

In their famous later observations in the Bank Wiring Room, the investigators studied the process by which a group of workers controlled the pace of work and the system of wage payment so as to produce results satisfactory to it *as a group* but unsatisfactory to management. They concluded, as against Taylor, that this kind of behaviour is not just the result of bad management—in the technical sense of controlling output and earnings—but the outcome of the group protecting itself *as a group* from what it perceives to be a hostile environment, i.e. the organization as a whole, or at least those members of it with whom they have close contact, the supervisor, the time study man, and so on.

As a result of the 'popularization' of the Hawthorne experiments, it is certain that managers have been influenced indirectly, perhaps unknowingly, by their results. They have been influenced even more, and more directly, by the writings of the theorists of formal organization. The ideas of Fayol in France, Mooney and Reilly in America and Urwick in Britain have gained widespread acceptance amongst managers, probably because their work was primarily directed towards the practical improvement of management. In so far as they were interested in theories of organization, it was to assist in this general improvement. Although they have much in common with Weber, these writers seem to have been entirely unaware of his work. Like Taylor they were practical men interested in the problems of their time, problems of large-scale organizations with complicated technologies. They were also interested to see how far the experience of large-scale organizations like armies was of relevance to the problems of industrial organization.

THEORISTS OF FORMAL ORGANIZATION: FAYOL AND URWICK

In the writings of Fayol and Urwick there are two interwoven strands which are very difficult to disentangle. One is the attempt at an abstract description of the elements of formal organization,* the other a set of practical guides to action in the design and management of organizations. The method of exposition these writers employed was to draw upon their own practical experience and that of others to define the salient features of efficient organization, and then to describe methods for the design and management of efficient organizations and some of the problems to be solved in the process.

Organizations exist for purposes, say Urwick[9] and Fayol[10]; they have objectives. Efficient organizations are precise in defining their objectives; they are also careful to look ahead to discern likely future happenings which will demand a re-formulation of objectives. Organizations must decide what activities have to be carried out to fulfil the objectives, and to assign these activities to persons. However, efficient organizations are careful not to define activities or to assign them by reference to particular individual persons. They define tasks impersonally taking into account the relation between the tasks and the problem of their co-ordination without reference to any existing persons. Having done so, they then think about the persons and the problems of fitting them to the jobs and relating them to other persons in other jobs. In short, they define the formal organization of jobs, and then try to fit people as closely as possible to them. It will never be a perfect fit, so the argument goes, human nature in general being what it is and individuals differing so much from one another.

There are in formal organizations, according to these theorists, problems of the distribution of authority, authority being defined as the power to require other persons to do things. There are also problems of equating authority with responsibility. That is to say, a person in a job must know what activities and resources of the organization and of other persons in it he is to be held accountable for and to whom; and he must be given power to get those things done for which he is held accountable. If he has less authority than responsibility he will not get things done efficiently. If he has more, then it is either redundant or dangerous or both, and certainly inefficient. Theorists of formal organization insist that power be distributed rationally in organizations,

*This term refers to those elements of organization which relate directly to organizational purposes and objectives and are designed to do so.

i.e. in the service of objectives. This must always be borne in mind when tasks are being assigned. Individuals must have no more power than is necessary for the efficient discharge of their duties.

Organizations, the formal organization theorists go on to say, employ specialists, persons who are 'authorities on' rather than having 'authority over'. Problems arise as to what ought to be the relationship between the 'authorities over' and the specialists. The efficient solution to this problem is to put the 'authorities over' into a chain of command, in which the areas of responsibility and the corresponding spread of authority diminish as one comes down the organization from the chief executive. The 'authorities on', the 'functional specialists', are not in this chain of command but are there to provide a technical service to it. If a technical function becomes a largish organization itself, as, for example, a design and development section, or a work study department, then it might have its own internal chain of command. On no account, however, must the authority within the specialist sub-organization cut across the main chain of command. This only leads to confusion and inefficiency.

One problem of the practical design of organizations is to decide how many persons one other person can effectively have under his authority, or, to put it the other way, how many can he efficiently be held responsible for—the problem of the span of control. This is really a part of the general problem of job or activity assignment. It has to do with co-ordination, and its corollary the problem of information flow. If one looks at the experience of large formal organizations with long chains of commands, such as armies and large industrial units, one finds, say the theorists of formal organization, that they are careful to have about six, certainly not more than ten, people answering to any one person.* Therefore, one ought to follow what has been found empirically to work and to construct one's organization accordingly.

The difficulty of disentangling theory from exhortation in the work of the theorists of formal organization is nowhere more marked than in the discussion of leadership and delegation, and its relation to the span of control. Leadership, if I have understood these writers, is to them a principle of organization. One would have thought it to be an attribute of persons, or a generalized description of a certain type of social behaviour. The organizational process which, we are told, accompanies the principle of leadership is the process of delegation.

*It has also been claimed that the efficient span of control can be mathematically calculated.

There is a temptation for a man in authority to take on too much responsibility himself. It is much more efficient to encourage in subordinates a sense of responsibility and this can only be done if they are assigned work, allowed to get on with it, and made accountable for it. Put like this, it would seem that the process of task assignment is something which becomes the prerogative of particular superiors in their search for organizational efficiency. The actual division of labour in an organization and the shape of the pyramid of command would, on this view, be the outcome of numerous personal decisions to delegate. Yet another view of the same assignment problem is that the tasks are allocated not by personal decision but in relation to objectives, and according to a master organizational plan. It may be that in a given firm both these processes go on.

Urwick in his book *The Elements of Administration*[9] says that he is using an engineering analogy in his analysis of organizations, because men are not sophisticated enough yet to understand and work with an organic one. It is useful, he says, to think about organization as a problem of design. And to some extent he discusses organizations in terms of questions like 'What is an organization for?' 'How does one put an organization together?' 'How does one keep it running?' But all the way through the discussion of problems of leadership, co-ordination and control, the inadequacy of the engineering model shows up. Not until recent years have sociologists and social psychologists shown the value of working consciously with an organic analogy. The work of the Hawthorne investigators was an important step in that direction, but it had little influence on theories of formal organization. In their theoretical ideas, the formal organization theorists were closer to Weber than to Elton Mayo. Their efficient organization is closely akin to a Weberian bureaucracy. Because of their practical bias they also raise, as Weber does not, many of the problems which arise for managers in the creation and in the maintenance of organizations. The theorists of formal organization do not, however, integrate these practical insights into their theoretical model very well. They are very interested in the question of the relationship of the individual, particularly the individual manager, to the organization, yet they make little use of the work of social psychologists and sociologists. They often discuss management very much in terms of practical flair; a business of using good judgement, picking up practical hints and so on. They do not seem to hold out much hope of the possibility that human behaviour in organizations might yield to systematic analysis and be susceptible to theoretical treatment. If human behaviour is problematical, this, they hint, is because of the effect of personal idiosyncrasy on formal organization.

The formal organization theorists, and Max Weber, have also been criticized for only having raised problems of organization without having proposed solutions to them. It is said, for example, that although we are told that there are problems about the best way to assign and co-ordinate tasks so that the ends of the organization are served and although the nature of these problems has been well defined, we are nowhere told just how these problems are to be solved in any given situation. One aspect of the assignment problem which is also frequently raised is whether and in what circumstances it is better to organize by process division or by product division. No answer is given to this one either, say the critics, only vague general practical hints to managers. The critics may well be right; yet it may still be claimed that Fayol, Urwick and others of the same school did a great service by identifying and stating clearly many of the problems of the design of formal organizations. They also indicated to managers, and commented wisely upon, the problems of authority, responsibility, leadership, delegation, and so on, which arise in the day-to-day running of an organization.

THE EMERGING SOCIAL SCIENCE OF ORGANIZATION

So far, in this discussion of the development of ideas of the nature of human organization for work, we have considered the contributions made by a group of social scientists with an interest in the practical problems of organization and management—the industrial psychologists and the Hawthorne investigators; and those made by a group of practical administrators interested in systematically presenting and theorizing about the problems of organization and management—Taylor and the scientific managers, and the theorists of formal organization. We also examined briefly some of Weber's ideas about the nature of modern bureaucracy. We are still left with many unanswered questions. Some attempts to answer these questions are described later in some detail. Here they are summarized briefly.

Some of the problems of the individual in relation to the organization were investigated by the Hawthorne researchers and the industrial psychologists. Theoretical developments in psychology now make it possible to speak with greater confidence about the nature of the human organism; and as we come to know more about the nature of organizations it is possible to say more about how the human organism might be affected by organizational procedures and controls. It is therefore possible now to suggest patterns of organization and management which will release individual potential. Amongst the chief contributors to the development of theories about the relation between the organization and the individual are Likert and his colleagues at the Social Science Research Centre at the University of Michigan, Argyris of Yale and McGregor of the Massachusetts Institute of Technology. Their ideas are based on carefully planned and executed research into the structure and functioning of organizations and the behaviour of individuals and groups within them. However, this work does not lack its critics and these will be mentioned later. The University of Michigan group has also researched into the relationship between supervisory style, productivity and the morale of working groups.

A neglected factor in the work we have so far discussed is technology. The industrial psychologists did concern themselves with problems of fatigue and boredom arising from repetitive work and the effect of this on output, but the effects of changes in technology on organizations and on the satisfaction and well-being of the people in them have until quite recently been relatively neglected. For example, the principles of organization and management proposed by the theorists of formal organization claimed universal applicability, regardless of the particular organizational setting in which they were applied. Weber's ideal type bureaucracy was also a kind of prototype for an efficient modern large-scale organization—governmental, industrial or commercial. Yet, now that it has been pointed out, it does not seem difficult to see that forms of organization appropriate to one purpose might be quite inappropriate to another, or that technology, i.e. the technical procedures and equipment available, might limit organizational alternatives, or that technology might play a large part in the process of human task definition and might place limits on human interaction and thus affect satisfaction and morale.* British researchers have played a leading role in the study of organization and technology, notably Burns of Edinburgh University,[11] Joan Woodward,[12] formerly of Liverpool

---

*The charge against social science that it is the pursuit of the obvious may with justice be answered by pointing out how the obvious is so often missed by managers and social scientists alike.

University, and Scott, Banks, Halsey and Lupton,[13] also of Liverpool. In America, Charles Walker[14] of Yale has studied the impact of assembly line technology on worker satisfaction and on patterns of supervision.

The study of social groups in industry, given impetus by the Hawthorne researches, has gone on. The University of Michigan team has worked on groups; so too have the Tavistock Institute of Human Relations and individuals in various universities in Britain and the U.S.A., e.g. Roy, formerly of Chicago University,[15] Lupton,[16] Cunnison,[17] and Wilson of Manchester, Sayles[18] of Columbia. The theoretical foundations for much of this work were laid by Lewin[19] and Homans.[20] Recently, deciding that enough was known about the structure and functioning of working groups to make fairly accurate prediction possible, Zaleznik and his colleagues at Harvard attempted with some success to do some predicting and they have published their results.[21]

It will have become clear that the emphasis has now shifted from armchair theorizing (Max Weber) and generalization from particular attempts at practical problems solving (Taylor, Fayol, etc.), to a concern with the scientific investigation of human behaviour in organizations. Since Hawthorne, most of the theoretical writing on organization and management has been done by practising social scientists from universities; not much by practising industrial managers. But in Britain the Chairman of the Glacier Metal Company, Wilfred Brown, has written much arising from his managerial experience and from the research which he has encouraged in his organization first by the Tavistock Institute and latterly by Dr Elliott Jaques.

Social scientists interested in the development of theory have come to publish their results for an audience of social scientists rather than for an audience of managers. This has sometimes meant that the practical relevance of their results has either not been examined at all, or has been missed because of difficulties of communication, or because of a confusion about what are problems of management and what are theoretical problems.

A good example of this is to be found in the work in the sociology of organizations which has followed from Max Weber. Robert Merton of Columbia University, amongst others, has criticized Weber on theoretical grounds, arguing that for various reasons an organization designed along the lines of Weber's ideal-type bureaucracy, would not necessarily be efficient.★ Merton[22] has argued, for example, that to define tasks and procedures in detail and to train people narrowly and intensively to perform them might render them (the people) incapable of adjusting easily to change. One of Merton's students, A. W. Gouldner, made an empirical study of an industrial firm where the process of bureaucratization was going on, and proposed, as a result, that Merton's theoretical ideas of 'bureaucratic dysfunction' were borne out by the facts of this case and that Weber's theoretical categories were too crude. He suggested how they might best be refined. A team of social scientists at Birmingham, following up theoretical leads from many disciplines, have recently worked out a scheme[23] for making operational† some of Weber's concepts, as a basis for the comparative study of organization structure and behaviour.

All this theoretical interchange can be very confusing to the manager who encounters it and who is asking what appear to be simple questions about how to handle change smoothly, what kinds of incentives are best, how to deal with the conflicts that crop up in the organization, why strikes happen and how can they be prevented, whether to organize by product or process, how to deal with the specialist in the organization, and so on. But neither the questions nor the answers are as simple as they appear.

Urwick may well have been right to say that people are not yet ready to discuss organization using organic analogues but would rather think of them as being like machines. If this is so, they are likely to be more confused than ever by current trends in sociology and organization theory. Pursuing the general problem of finding organizational alternatives which will give a good balance of advantage between economic, technical and human satisfactions in organizations (which is after all the major problem confronting managers and from which most others derive), social scientists have been using increasingly the analogue of an organism in a changing environment. It has proved possible in this way to clarify problems of decision making—for example, choosing appropriate policies to allow the organization to remain in equilibrium with its environment, while at the same time finding the right balance of technological, economic and human satisfactions. It is also possible to make sense of some of the many problems of tension and conflict which emerge as a result of technological and

★This criticism would also apply to the principles of the formal organization theorists.
†i.e. defining them so that they can be isolated and measured.

administrative change. The role–personality problem makes more sense also in this framework and so does the relation of formal and informal organization. The organic model, which has shown itself a useful aid in the analysis of practical problems of managerial decision making, derives partly from social anthropology, partly from psychology, and has been developed as an aid to organizational analysis by Rice and Trist of the Tavistock Institute, and by March, Cyert and Simon of the Carnegie Institute of Technology at Pittsburgh, amongst others. Their work will be discussed more fully in Part IV.

The position and standing of the social science of industrial organization as I see it is as follows. Many of the ideas which were generated by the Hawthorne experiments, by Taylor and the Industrial Psychologists, either have been translated into techniques which are widely used, or by popularization have become part of the normal mode of thought of many managers. The same is true of the work of the formal organization theorists. While this process has been going on, an increasing number of social scientists have become interested in industry as a field for research, and have become extremely critical of the methods and the conclusions of earlier workers. They have developed more refined methods of investigation and analysis. A very large number of individual and group researches have been carried out in the U.S.A., in Britain and in France. The findings will obviously have some practical value, but at the moment there is still work of popular diffusion to do, and a theoretical job of integrating the results of many researches into a comprehensive theory of organization. We can now go on to discuss some of these researches and point to their practical consequences.

II

Testing the Theory:
Some Individual Studies

Testing the Theory:
Some Individual Studies

The social scientist in industry works at his job of adding to knowledge in his subject using much the same approach as the physical scientist. He knows that many people have attempted to explain the causes and consequences of human behaviour in industry; some by trying to generalize from practical experience, others by systematic research, yet others by armchair theorizing; and he gets to know this work well. He takes some of the explanations which have been proposed, subjects them to logical criticism, and puts them in a form in which they can be tested against facts about human behaviour in industry systematically observed. He then observes and tests. His contribution to practical affairs is measured by the extent to which, as a result of his work, it becomes possible more accurately to explain and predict the outcome of particular human activities in industrial organizations.

A STUDY OF INDUSTRIAL BUREAUCRACY

It will be recalled that Max Weber and the theorists of formal organization held that efficiency was largely the outcome of careful attention to formal organization. Their ideas can easily be formulated as '*if . . . then
. . .*' statements. *If* you have clear rules and roles, systematic procedures for selection, training and promotion, the right span of control, etc., etc., *then* you will be making the best use of the resources which are available to you, in pursuit of the ends you desire. This is a fairly widely held belief amongst managers, although it is often qualified by statements about the frailty and human cussedness which interfere with the rational pursuit of those objectives which managers regard as desirable.

Gouldner, an American sociologist, some years ago decided to examine some of the ideas which are explicit and implicit in Weber's bureaucratic model, by reference to the facts. My purpose in summarizing his studies here is to show their bearing on the empirical truth or falsity of these propositions, and then to draw practical conclusions.

Weber said that bureaucracies were governed by impersonal rules. Gouldner points out that Weber paid little attention to the question of who makes the rules and to the process by which they are made. Common experience suggests that this is an important question in industry. Whether the rules which govern behaviour are arbitrarily imposed or jointly agreed might have a great deal to do with efficiency. If it seems odd that Weber chose to ignore an obviously important question it should be remembered that he drew his examples mainly from the civil service. The relation between participation in the rules set up to govern behaviour, industrial behaviour itself, and efficiency, is one which people in industry have strong views about. It is surely useful then to examine this relationship in the light of the facts and try to get nearer the truth. This is Gouldner's method. Gouldner also noticed that Weber had skated over questions about the ends served by particular rules and their usefulness as seen by different persons and groups in an organization. There might well be conflict about goals and the rules and procedures designed to serve them. As Gouldner argues, Weber seems to be interested in structure almost to the exclusion of social process. The concept of bureaucracy is a static concept. It is pertinent to ask what factors contribute to the persistence or otherwise of bureaucratic forms. There seems to be ground for doubt whether organizations which are bureaucratic in form are necessarily efficient. It might, therefore, be begging the question to say that they survive in that form because they are efficient. The social and political pressure towards bureaucratic forms and their maintenance may not arise exclusively from a desire for technical efficiency but for other reasons. It was with such questions in mind that Gouldner embarked upon his study of a Gypsum factory in the U.S.A.

It would be tedious to repeat arguments of social scientists about the scientific value of studies of particular cases, but a brief word is necessary on this. There is substance in the criticism which points to the dangers of generalizing from the facts of a single case, but at this stage in the development of industrial sociology there is much to be said for the study of single cases. In trying to identify significant variables it is useful to get close to the data, to know one organization well. Then if it appears possible to isolate and measure particular variables and to propose hypotheses about the relations between them, it might be worth embarking upon wider comparative studies. Gouldner studied with his colleagues one small factory of 225 people off and on for about three years. The plant was in a small semi-rural community where kinship still meant a great deal and where relationships in the community tended to be carried over into the plant and vice versa. The men employed at the factory were parochial in their attitudes and loyalties. They distrusted the head office people and the union organizers from the big city. This shared distrust of outside agencies helped cement relationships in the plant. Relations between managers, supervisors and workers were in consequence personal, informal, governed much more by custom and practice than by formal rule.

Even before the study began, this pattern was beginning to break up. Head office, faced with more tightly competitive markets, was beginning to ask questions about the efficiency of the plant and what might be done to improve it. In two books[24, 25] reporting his research Gouldner describes the process of bureaucratization, its causes and consequences. The situation as he found it before head office moved in to tighten things up was summed up by the term 'Indulgency pattern'. The workers who were interviewed were unanimous in saying that the management and the supervisors were not strict. There was a good deal of informal job changing, a blind eye was turned to certain kinds of pilfering, selection of workers for jobs was organized on the basis of friendship and kinship as much as on formal qualification. Promotion procedures operated similarly. Starting and finishing time and coffee breaks were loosely interpreted, and so on.

The workmen valued this pattern. They resented the idea that managers and supervisors should exert authority for its own sake but were conscious of a technical obligation, i.e. they were happy to accept discipline when it was seen to relate directly to production. The pattern of supervision allowed the men a great deal of control over their working environment and this they liked. They also valued the fact that relationships within the plant were not entirely governed by the formal requirements of production, but by sentiments such as might be typical of neighbourliness or friendship in a non-industrial context.

In an earlier section describing the Hawthorne experiments the idea of the industrial organization as a social system was introduced. The general characteristic of a system is that all the parts are related to one another in such a way that a change in one will have repercussions on all others. Any attempt, therefore, to impose a system akin to Weber's bureaucracy or the formal organization of Fayol and Urwick upon one where relationships rest upon tradition, custom and sentiment, might be expected to generate resentment and opposition, however rational those who impose the system see it to be.

Gouldner describes in detail the consequences of the attempted bureaucratization of the plant by a new manager appointed by the head office of the company with instructions to make the plant more efficient. The new man quickly broke up the indulgency pattern. He introduced other newcomers into managerial and supervisory jobs and instituted new procedures of formal control, e.g. work study, production control, paperwork reporting systems, more formal procedures of selection for jobs and checks on pilfering. These measures threatened to break up the well-established pattern of mutual rights, duties and obligations; to make things worse, they were being imposed by outsiders. The system reacted and the first effect was one of tension, relieved by behaviour inimical to the demands of the new regime. To counter this, the new regime resorted to closer supervision with new supervisors. But close supervision merely generated further tension.

The point Gouldner emphasizes is this: the new man could neither accept nor adjust to the indulgency pattern and at the same time meet the expectations of his superiors. In any case, being an outsider as well as a successor to the position of chief executive in the factory, the process of adjustment would for him have taken a long time and time was not on his side. Bureaucracy, says Gouldner, might very well be the only alternative open to a managerial successor to control an organization in this kind of situation. Yet, it might generate tension and resistance. Control might then only be possible by more bureaucratic procedures, and so more tension is generated. Therefore, it is not really helpful and practical to advise managers, as do the theorists of formal organization and the scientific managers, that if you want efficiency you must pay attention to formal organization. One really wants to know the likely effects of such changes in terms of efficiency, and this in turn means that one must understand the kind of system one is tampering with. Without such knowledge it is impossible to predict the outcome. Nor is it wise to expect that a mere change of managerial personnel will do, because a tendency to impose bureaucratic measures seems to be inherent in the role of the successor. Again, the consequences are difficult to predict unless one has a way of analysing and describing the existing system.

In the Gypsum factory the consequence of bureaucracy was a series of bitter disputes and an unofficial strike. Gouldner attributes this type of reaction not to personal ham-fistedness by the new manager, nor to bloody-mindedness and nostalgia by the workers, although these were some surface manifestations of difficulty, but rather to the attempt to disturb a stable and highly valued ongoing system of relationships. The practical conclusion to be drawn from this is that it might be wise to try to understand and to work with an existing and stable pattern of relationships if one wishes to effect change smoothly. This sounds so obvious as to be hardly worth saying; yet it is clear from Gouldner's work that there is great pressure upon a successor to a managerial role to make changes in the direction of bureaucratization and to break up customary and traditional patterns, largely because it is difficult quickly to break into them. The consequences of bureaucratization in such circumstances might well run counter to the productive efficiency which is aimed at. New job definitions, new procedures and new styles of supervision will be subjected, consciously or otherwise, to the questions: 'Does it fit my/our interest?' 'Does it offend against the things I/we have come to value?' 'Does it make me/us feel comfortable and satisfied in my/our mind?' 'Does it seem likely to affect my/our future adversely?' If the answers to these questions for an individual or a group are not satisfactory, it is useless to argue that the new system is right because it leads to productive efficiency 'which is what everybody wants', because this will be seen as yet another attempt to impose the kind of change which is already resented. So while it might be obvious that it is sensible to work with an existing and valued system as far as possible, one's success in doing so will rest upon one's capacity to analyse and predict. It is certainly not enough to say that attention to formal organization plus a ready tongue and human sympathy is all the equipment a manager needs. He needs some tools for the analysis of social systems. These, rather than general practical hints, are what the social scientist can best provide.

Gouldner shows, in his analysis of the Gypsum factory, how useful the notion of *role expectations* can be, in explaining how human behaviour in organizations is influenced and controlled. Regularity and predictability in social relationships are highly valued by individuals. They expect that the persons they associate with, at work or in the family, will behave in predictable ways. If they do not, the individual feels tense and uncomfortable and wants to do something to make life more predictable. In all human groupings there are mechanisms for punishing people who do not behave in predictable ways and for rewarding those who do. Gradually, the norms of behaviour which emerge from the desire for predictability became part of the individual's personal make-up. He sometimes does not know how to explain why he behaves regularly in the way he does. It's just 'the way we do things here'. In short, people cast other people in roles which are defined by their own expectations. These may be highly formal, as legal prescriptions and bureaucratic rules are, or they may be informal or implicit, as in custom. Because of the urge to predictability, role expectations, whether formal or informal, tend towards stable equilibrium in social systems and there is pressure for them to remain that way. This is one reason why imposed social change, say as a result of new technology, may be a difficult problem. In a later section we shall examine some of the problems of technical change from this standpoint. In the next two studies we will see the way in which technology affects role expectations and human satisfactions, and the processes by which groups attempt to control their environment to satisfy the interests and values of their members. And we shall have some new tools of analysis to introduce.

ASSEMBLY LINE TECHNOLOGY AND THE WORKER

Walker and Guest in their book *The Man on the Assembly Line*[14] report an investigation into the factors in assembly line work which promote satisfaction or dissatisfaction with the job. This study is in the tradition of Industrial Psychology but it takes full account of much of the work which has been done in Social Psychology and Sociology since the classical studies of boredom, monotony and fatigue carried out in Britain during and after the first world war. It is concerned to trace the effects of a particular kind of production technology, the assembly line, on the attitudes of workers to their jobs.

In assembly line technology, the pace is controlled mechanically, the work being brought to the worker and taken away on completion, usually by mechanical means. The total job of assembling a motor-car, for example, is broken down minutely into repetitive tasks. Each individual task needs little skill and is easily learned. The tools and the techniques to be used are not determined or chosen by the worker but by the engineers who design the line. Typically, assembly line jobs do not require close and continuous and deep mental attention, but neither will they perform themselves. They need, as Walker and Guest put it, 'surface mental attention'. The questions which these investigators asked were: *as seen by the worker himself*, what are the effects on job satisfaction, of his immediate job, his relations with his fellow workers and the supervisors, his pay and security, his working conditions, the arrangements for promotion and transfer and relations with his trade union?

Like Gouldner's research, this is a study of one case, a new and up-to-date motor-car final assembly plant in a town of more traditional industry. This situation was chosen for study because the final assembly of vehicles is the example *par excellence* of assembly line work. In this particular case the men on the assembly line had recent experience of more traditional technologies with which to make comparison. A total of 180 workers were interviewed and their attitudes systematically recorded and analysed.

The great majority of the men interviewed in the plant had no previous experience of anything remotely resembling line work, so that they were evaluating a fairly fresh experience. However, not all of their jobs contained the same mixture of elements. Some were on a moving conveyor, others not; some were highly repetitive, others less so; the change of experience differed from man to man. However, when each worker was questioned about his job he seemed to single out the elements of mechanical pacing and repetitiveness as being particularly irksome and unsatisfying. There were exceptions. A minority positively liked mechanical pacing and its concomitants. This was also found in earlier studies, some of which are summarized in Georges Friedmann's book *Industrial Society*.[26] The majority of workers with mechanically paced, repetitive jobs of low skill put their immediate job at the top of the list of things they disliked about their total situation in the plant, although they were highly satisfied with the pay and with the security which the job offered.

It has recently come to be more generally recognized that the technology of manufacture helps shape the pattern of interpersonal relations on the job. This seems obvious enough, and yet when one examines the work of the theorists of formal organization one finds scant recognition of its significance. An extreme example of this effect is the solitary individual who sits in a control room watching dials. For most of his time at work he has no interpersonal relations. In assembly line work the effect of the design of the line on the pattern of interaction is clear. The way in which the engineers break down the job and specify the time cycle of operations and physical movements, will determine the functional relationships between jobs and what opportunities will exist for conversation and other forms of social interaction. Physical conditions, such as the noise level, will set limits to the extent to which those opportunities will be utilized. In turn, all this will have its effect on the extent to which an individual feels a sense of identity with a social grouping and hence might colour his attitude to the job and to the company he works for.

In the factory studied by Walker and Guest there were some jobs which provided opportunities for social interaction where conditions, e.g. the noise level, made it possible for individuals to exploit them. The men who did these jobs perceived these social aspects of their jobs as desirable, just as those who held jobs which entailed social isolation regarded this as undesirable. When one considers that a little more than half of the workers interviewed had jobs of the latter kind one is led to conclude either that it is the nature of assembly line technology to inhibit valued social interaction, or that it might be possible if this element of job satisfaction were to enter into the calculations of the designers, so to design the jobs and layouts as to remove these inhibitions, while at the same time retaining the technical advantages of the method. Similarly, it might well be possible to look at individual jobs to see whether it is possible to make them less rigidly paced and repetitive and not lose output, by 'job enlargement' for example. Walker and Guest make both these points and they have been emphasized by other social scientists. In my experience they are rarely taken into account by the engineers who design assembly lines.

Just as the technology of assembly line production helps shape the pattern of social interaction on the job, so it imposes limits on promotion opportunities and influences the relationship between the worker and his supervisor and managers. One of the objectives of assembly line work is to reduce all jobs to a minimum skill level. This maximizes its technical and administrative advantages. Yet, to the extent that uniformity of skill and payment for it are achieved, so the opportunities are limited for individuals to move from jobs of low pay, status and skill to jobs at a higher level, simply because there are no such jobs on the shop floor. The men Walker and Guest interviewed saw this as being of importance in their assessment of their jobs. However, in the particular plant studied there were opportunities to transfer from highly paced repetitive jobs to others less so; people liked this because their motive for wanting to move from job to job was not, on the whole, higher pay and status but escape from monotony and fatigue. Workers did not only *say* that certain elements in the job were unsatisfactory, they 'voted with their feet'. Absenteeism and turnover were related positively to elements in the job such as machine pacing, repetitiveness and social deprivation. Satisfaction found its expression in behaviour as well as in attitude.

The view is, I think, fairly common amongst managers, that good lighting and ventilation and good welfare services are important elements in job satisfaction. Possibly this view has emerged because often it is draughts and canteen food that workers officially complain about. Walker and Guest's findings on this have been amply confirmed by other investigators. They found that while good general working conditions are appreciated by workers, when looked at in relation to other factors in the job such as pay and security and machine control, they do not occupy a prominent place in job satisfaction.

Another effect of assembly line technology is that the role of supervisors and managers is defined in a special way. Workers see a lot of the supervisors, whose job requires them to keep a constant eye on the assembly line to ensure that it keeps running continuously. They see little of the managers of the plant who are preoccupied with questions wider than the detailed technical and human co-ordination of shop floor work. The workers interviewed by Walker and Guest reported that they saw a lot of their supervisors, thought that this relationship was important in job satisfaction, and on the whole were satisfied with their particular supervisors. They hardly ever saw the managers and did not regard relationships with them of importance. Walker and Guest compare this with the situation in the steel industry where there is a much more frequent and important relationship with management, which seems to arise out of the imperatives of steel-making technology.

I have left Walker and Guest's findings about the place of wages and job security until last not because these are unimportant. I just wished to offset the usual exclusive concern with these, by an emphasis on some other aspects of job satisfaction. I have also been anxious to establish the general importance of technology as a shaper of social structure and job definition, and to point out that variations of social structure and job definition might well be possible within the limits set by a particular technology, using the findings of *The Man on the Assembly Line* to exemplify this. In fact pay and security are of great importance in job satisfaction. A majority of workers were attracted to the assembly plant from other jobs largely because it offered much higher wages and greater security. On average, workers had gained about 50 per cent in weekly income by moving. When weighing the things they liked and disliked about the assembly line job, 80 per cent of those interviewed placed economic factors first in their list of 'likes'. And most men also placed security high.

It has become something of a fashion these days to question the value of trades unions to working men. Some economists argue that they are futile because they have no long-term effect on the general level of real wages. It has also been said that since employers are now becoming more aware of the economic advantages of having a satisfied labour force, there is less need for unions. Walker and Guest questioned the men on the job. Two-thirds of them were in favour of the union. It proved to be useful in handling grievances arising from the unsatisfactory elements in the job. By bringing these problems to the notice of management, improvements were initiated. The researchers concluded that membership of the union helped counterbalance the impersonality and anonymity in the job. However, the existence of a union was not seen by the men as a powerful factor affecting their like or dislike of the situation as a whole.

Walker and Guest offer us an analysis which combines the approach of the psychologist to the effects on the worker of physical conditions of work. the social psychologist who is interested in the effect on the individual of membership of a social grouping, and the sociologist whose concern is with the factors which influence the structuring of social relationships. From a slightly different standpoint their research examines some aspects of the problems which interested Gouldner, namely, the factors which influence task-definition and the rules which govern relationships at work. In the case of assembly line work, technology obviously plays a major part in bureaucratizing shop-floor relationships. It also affects the structure of management and its relations with the shop floor. Yet even assembly-line technology is not entirely limiting. Walker and Guest conclude their study by pointing to the ways in which the technology itself and the administrative arrangements for wage payment, transfer, promotion, etc., offer opportunities to management to search for alternative layouts and procedures which balance economic, technical and social satisfactions. We shall be looking more closely to see what support research gives to this general proposition. At this point it will be helpful to follow the lead offered by Walker and Guest, by turning to a British study made after the second world war which, instead of examining one case, has compared the influence on organizations of different production technologies. I refer to the preliminary summary of the results which has appeared in Miss Joan Woodward's *Management and Technology*.[12]

THE INFLUENCE OF PRODUCTION TECHNOLOGY UPON ORGANIZATION

In introducing Miss Woodward's work it is worth mentioning that when it appeared it threw advocates of theories of formal organization into some disarray. It will be recalled that these theories discuss the efficiency of organization mostly in terms of formal means to co-ordinate tasks which have been assigned as parts of a total task or objective, and they generalize about these formal means without reference to the particular tasks involved, or to the technical means employed. Studies which spread doubt by purporting to show that the technology of manufacture itself constitutes a limit on possible organization are therefore a challenge to established theory. The proponents of established theory are fighting a rearguard action. Usefully, because there are parts of their territory which are worth defending.

Miss Woodward's avowed aim in her research was:

> 'to discover whether the principles of organization laid down by an expanding body of management theory correlate with business success when put into practice'.[27]

In particular she intended to look at the relationship between line managers and specialists. It soon became clear to her that this relationship could not be studied in isolation. When comparing data collected in 100 firms in the south-east of England it emerged that considerable variations in size, type of industry or success in business were not clearly related to patterns of organization. Yet when the firms were grouped according to similarity of objective and technology of manufacture, there did appear to be a relation between technology and organizational pattern or structure.

The firms in the sample were placed into ten different categories according to their production system. Roughly, they fell into three larger technological divisions with some slight overlap: small batch and unit production, large batch and mass production, and process production. The ten production groups form a crude scale of technical complexity, technical complexity being defined in terms of the degree of control over production and predictability of results. The general conclusion was that organizational patterns differed at different levels of technical complexity. For example, the number of levels in the managerial hierarchy increased with technical complexity. The span of control of the first line supervisor increased along the scale and reached its peak under mass production. It then declined through the process technologies. Process production seems to demand a very much higher ratio of managers to other personnel than other types of technology. Ratios of direct to indirect labour, the proportion of university graduates amongst supervisory staff, and the span of control of the chief executive all increase as one moves along the scale from low to high technical complexity. In Miss Woodward's sample, specialization of function in management appears to be found more frequently in batch and mass production firms. In unit production firms, there were few specialists. In process firms, the line managers were also technical specialists.

Miss Woodward also found that it was in the large batch and mass production firms that the actual administration of production by modern techniques of production scheduling and control, work study, and so on, was the most widely separated from the personal supervision of production. Thus the solutions advanced by Taylor for production efficiency seem to be adopted efficiently over a certain range of technologies, but are not universally applicable. *Management and Technology* indicates that one would be wise to examine every prescription for improved organization with the question in mind, 'Is it appropriate to this technology?' This makes life much more complicated perhaps than the theorists of formal organization were ready to admit; but then life *is* complicated.

Already, having looked at the findings of Walker and Guest, we would expect technology to have its effect on job satisfaction and the quality of relationships. Miss Woodward looks along the scale of technological complexity for evidence of changes in this respect. She finds a relation between technical complexity, as measured on her scale, and what she describes as 'the attitudes and behaviour of management and supervisory staff and the tone of industrial relations'. At both ends of the scale, pressures on people from technology seemed to be less than they were in the middle of the scale. That is to say that generally the atmosphere was more relaxed and people liked it better in one-off technologies and process technologies, than in the batch and mass-production technologies. It is worth pointing out, perhaps, that this could mean that great personal skill in leadership, delegation, and so on, which is emphasized so much by the theorists of formal organization, might pay much worse dividends in efficiency and satisfaction in some technological settings than in others. This does not, of course, minimize their importance. It merely warns us not to treat them as isolated causes of efficiency or satisfaction.

The main argument of *Management and Technology*, from the standpoint of the practising manager, is that there seems to be a pattern of organization appropriate to the technology employed. Or, to put it another way, the technology demands certain forms of organization for its efficient exploitation. In building up organizations, which can be, as the theorists of organization point out, a deliberate act of planning, one should try to be sensitive to technological demands. In her research, for example, Miss Woodward found some firms which had consciously followed the theories of formal organization and had become inefficient in consequence because they were inappropriate technologically, successful firms which had consciously adapted organization to technology, and unsuccessful ones which had made no attempt at organization building, but which had spontaneously grown an organization pattern out of the relationships between particular influential individuals, which was inappropriate and inefficient. There is probably a fourth category of firms which spontaneously adapt to the demands of technology and are successful.

Other studies of management and technology seem to confirm the point made in *Management and Technology*. A study by Tom Burns[11] elaborates the general point that a flexible *organic* kind of organization is most appropriate to firms in situations of rapidly changing objectives and technology, and a more formal *mechanical* kind of organization will work well where objectives and technology are well established and not subject to rapid change.

Miss Woodward's work has been criticized because the classification of production technology is crude, and because of her excessive emphasis on one variable—technology and its relation to organization. But hers was one very useful starting point not only for a critical look at the prescriptions of formal organization theory but also for future researches, some of which we shall examine later.

It will now be interesting to ask what problems emerge when technology changes radically and quickly in the same organization.

TECHNICAL AND ADMINISTRATIVE CHANGE

The resistance which is sometimes offered to the introduction of new methods of doing work in organizations, e.g. new machinery or new administrative procedures, is often thought to be due to something called 'the inherent conservatism of man'. This is to say, in effect, that the resistance is a property of human nature. Were this so, then it would not seem possible to effect changes without changing human nature. Yet we are also told that 'human nature cannot be changed'. Are we to admit, therefore, that nothing can be done? Surely not, because it is known to common sense that there are some situations of change where little in the way of resistance is encountered, and others where there is much. This seems to suggest that resistance to change might have to be explained by reference to the properties of situations rather than to the properties of individuals. But of course both are relevant. Indeed, it is hardly possible to speak of one without referring to the other.

When we were discussing Gouldner's work we saw how a disturbance of stable customary expectations, embedded as these are in existing interpersonal relationships, generates resistance to administrative changes. The individual in such situations is attempting to adapt to his social environment so as to maintain his own psychological equilibrium. In doing so he might resist what are perceived as disturbing changes— 'the inherent conservatism of man'; but the social situation, that is his relationships with others, the social norms which govern them, and the shared interests with like folk which are associated with them, will deeply influence the way the individual interprets the change—and what he regards as disturbing. In Gouldner's factory, the workers felt that the 'indulgency pattern' which they valued was being threatened, and from this emerged the resistance to measures of bureaucracy. Different groups, according to their particular situation, offered their own particular brands of resistance.

The reader will have discerned by now that social science theory holds that stable and customary expectations are built up from a number of ingredients. For example, the structure of relationships between persons in organizations is partly shaped by technology (Woodward,

Walker and Guest, etc.) which defines the required functional inter-action. It is also partly shaped by the administrative procedures which are necessary to make the technological system function and which link the organization to its external environment—to its customers, to government, and so on (Weber, Gouldner). Also, the structure may be influenced by the deliberate acts of powerful individuals, who set objectives and assign tasks. But all these influences only create as it were the bony framework of organization. They specify the jobs which need to be done, who will work with whom, for what purpose and under whose direction. The possible shape of the framework is, as we have seen, limited but not completely determined by the constraints of technology (Woodward). But the way in which the framework 'comes to life' is through the activities of individuals in their interpersonal relationships.

We shall describe in a later section the processes by which groups form and create their own norms and sanctions to ensure conformity to those norms. For the moment it is sufficient to say that social groups form in organizations when people who work near each other, and are functionally interdependent, elaborate their relationships beyond the formal requirements of the organization. The result is sometimes re-ferred to as the 'informal' organization although this does not describe it well. As groups elaborate their relationships, norms and social con-trols, they try like individuals to get into some kind of stable equili-brium with the immediate environment, that is to say with other nearby groups, with the authority system of the organization, and so on. In some situations this process results in behaviour by the group which is inimical to the purposes of the organization as formally de-fined, and we have the familiar 'restrictive practice'. In other cases this does not happen. It is of great practical importance to find some explanation for this difference. There are two recent British researches which have explored the problems of technological change, the Liverpool University study *Technical Change and Industrial Relations*,[13] and the study from the Tavistock Institute, *Organizational Choice*.[28] The detailed theory of the working group which is relevant to the problems of industrial change and efficiency will be examined by reference to the work of an American Sociologist, Donald Roy,[15] and to my own book *On the Shop Floor*.[16]

The Liverpool workers chose as their field of study a large steel plant, with what appeared to be a remarkable history of smooth assimilation to large-scale technical changes. The research was designed to analyse the impact upon the social structure of the plant of various technical changes which had taken place and others which were currently in hand. Their objective was twofold, to add generally to knowledge about organizations and their problems and to try to identify in this particular case the factors which had encouraged the smooth assimilation of change. The research had a historical dimension. It was expected that the experience of previous changes and the persistence of certain patterns of relationships formed in the past, might do much to explain current behaviour in the face of change or impending change.

The plant in question manufactured sheet steel. It was the major industrial plant in a small community. When the study was undertaken in 1953 there were 7,000 employees. In 1896 there had been 250 men under the personal control of the owner. The growth of the plant was accompanied by, and was partly a consequence of, both technical changes and backward integration towards the raw materials. Not only had the plant grown; the occupational composition of its working force had changed remarkably and this seemed to be largely due to the technical changes. For example, as a result of the introduction of labour-saving machinery, the percentage of direct production workers fell from 82 per cent of the working force to 65 per cent in the period from 1925 to 1953. At the same time, owing to the growing technical complexity of the processes, the percentage of people engaged in maintenance and service jobs increased more than twofold. Probably because of the administrative problems of control arising from increasing size and technical complexity, the percentage of administrative staff also doubled over the period.

The original steel rolling process employed in the plant was the 'Staffordshire Mill', and the growth of the firm consisted in the addition of more mills, each operated by a team of ten men. This mode of expansion had no effect on occupational structure nor did it give rise to difficult managerial problems of control, because each team was largely self-contained and self-governing and was paid a wage based on the team output. In the very early years of the plant's history the leader of each team was in fact a sub-contractor to the firm. It was when the company decided to make its own steel for rolling, and later to make its own iron, then to introduce revolutionary changes in the methods of steel making and sheet rolling, that the division of labour became complicated and management and control difficult. This had consequences for the structuring of management organization, for the type of manager required and for the patterning of shop-floor relationships. The detailed analysis of the history of the relation between technical change and social structure in this steel plant amply confirms the suspected existence of a very strong connexion between technology, the structure of occupations, the formal structuring of work relations and informal organization.

Trades unions represent the interests of various occupational groupings. In plants like this one, which had two unions sharing the organization of the process workers and fifteen unions organizing the various maintenance and service workers, there were and are problems arising from the impact of changing occupational structure on the spheres of influence of the unions. These problems and the methods used for their solution were also analysed in detail by the Liverpool researchers.

All these analyses confirmed the first general impression that technical change had, in fact, been assimilated without major difficulty. There had been many serious problems arising for example from the complete disappearance of some occupations—like the 'Staffordshire Mill' operators, from the reduction in the proportion of men required to run the processes, from the increasing growth in the numbers and importance of the maintenance and service workers, as the plant became technically and administratively more complex. There were also problems of redundancy, transfer and re-training; problems of bonus rates, shiftwork rotas, wage differentials, trade union demarcation, and so on. Yet for all this, there was an absence of overt resistance to change, or of unmanageable conflict accompanying it. Why? What caused industrial peace in this plant? The researchers adduce several reasons for this, some of them directly related to the technology of steel making, others relating less directly and having to do with the administrative mechanisms for the redress of grievances and for the handling of management–worker relations. There are yet others which appear to be even less related to technological factors. These have to do with the relations between the plant and the local community.

Steel making and rolling is typically controlled by teams of operators, as for example on a 'Staffordshire Mill', where ten men worked in close co-ordination, each with his own clearly defined job, and in dirty and dangerous circumstances. The same may be said of the open hearth steel furnace crew or the blast furnace crew, or even the crew of a modern strip mill, although there are differences in detail. These teams differentiate their members by function; they also arrange themselves in hierarchical order of skill and authority. Traditionally, boys are recruited from school to the lower ranks of these team hierarchies; as the years pass, they go step by step up the ladder, learning the job and accumulating seniority, until they become leading hands with high responsibility and high pay. Once having started to mount the ladder in a particular plant it is impossible for a man to transfer to another steel factory laterally. Therefore it is in his long-term interest to remain with the same company because he has a personal stake in it and in its survival. This tendency was reinforced in the plant studied (and this has been shown to be the case in other steel plants) by the mode of recruitment of young workers from the local community through the network of kinship, and by the tradition of allowing the trade union branches to adjudicate on seniority claims. Therefore there was much to generate attitudes of loyalty and identification with the company.

These considerations did not apply so strongly to the maintenance men. They do not work in functionally diversified hierarchical crews but individually or with 'mates' or peers. For them there is no promotion by seniority. The skill of the craftsman is transferable and 'lateral' movement is possible. The Liverpool researchers found that a much greater proportion of the craft force were immigrants to the area, they had fewer kinship ties, and their unions at national level were much less closely identified with the industry than the process workers' unions. The craftsmen had much less of a stake in the company, and their unions less of a stake in the industry. Therefore, it was to be expected that they would take a somewhat different attitude to changes initiated by management and exploit their powerful position, which was what happened.

By contrast, the machinery for negotiation and redress of grievances, developed by the process workers' unions and the employers, treats the shop-floor delegate as an important participant and gives him much power at shop-floor level. This machinery, which is highly valued, has helped to avoid overt conflict erupting from differences of opinion within the plant.

The informal relaxed atmosphere between manager and manager and between the workers and management seemed to have persisted in spite of the increasing size and complexity of the plant and the entry of technical specialists into management from outside. This also helped the process of assimilating change. Woodward noted in her study the way in which process technologies seem conducive to a relaxed atmosphere in industrial relations.

Steel is also an industry of low labour costs. It has, therefore, been possible for management to make concessions on wage and manning questions without adding much to the cost of the product. This has undoubtedly contributed in the past to cordial worker and union co-operation with management and has helped to get change accepted. Finally, the technology of steel making is such that change takes a long time to implement. Plant takes years to build and this allows time to plan. Given the predisposition of managers and unions to talk, many of the problems of change can be anticipated and dealt with.

The Liverpool study shows that although the effects of technological innovation may be to change radically the social structure, it is possible, given time and appropriate machinery for the redress of grievances, to assimilate it smoothly. Because of technology and location some steel plants are particularly fortunately placed, and their traditions help. Other plants in other industries might find life less pleasant. Yet it seems clear that if they will analyse the effects of technology on their social structure, using a socio-psychological frame, they might be able better to predict the problems that change will bring and to assess whether the machinery of redress is efficient enough to cope with them, and what needs to be done to make it so. Certainly the kind of analyses which have been described in this section would be helpful.

A point is made implicitly in the Liverpool study, namely, that the efficient handling of technological change by management is a matter of finding solutions to problems which will minimize the disturbance to the existing social structure, in so far as it is already providing satisfaction, and which will maximize the economic and technical benefits of the change. *Organizational Choice* makes the point explicitly and in so doing improves upon the theoretical conceptions of the Liverpool study.

Organizational Choice is a report of researches carried out in coal mines by a group of social scientists. The approach they adopted is one they and their fellow workers at the Tavistock Institute of Human Relations had developed over a number of years. In this approach, a production system can be usefully regarded as comprising a technical organization—that is, machines and equipment deployed in given ways—and a work organization relating to the persons who perform the necessary tasks. Although the work organization is limited by the technology, it also has social and psychological properties of its own which are independent of technology. The production system comprising these two elements has also to satisfy certain economic criteria. The problem of relating organizations effectively and stably to the environments in which they operate is one of trying to balance the economic, technological and socio-psychological advantages. The hypothesis proposed is that to optimize any one of these elements does not necessarily result in a set of conditions optimal for the system as a whole. To strive for maximum technical advantage and economic reward might well create social and psychological havoc, which in turn jeopardizes economic goals. Similarly, to attempt to create high job satisfaction might adversely affect the gain to be had from technological efficiency, and so on.

Once one has become used to the way social scientists think about industrial organizations, one does not find this a surprising hypothesis to propose. Yet it would certainly not have been proposed in this form by any of the writers whom we discussed in the first part of this essay; by Taylor, for example, who thought that everything followed from technical efficiency, or by the theorists of formal organization who stressed the importance of the work organization, or by Hawthorne investigators who emphasized morale and job satisfaction. But most of the researches which have been carried out by sociologists and social psychologists lead to a conception of the industrial organization as a system with the three major elements closely interwoven.

With these ideas in mind, the investigators studied the processes of mechanization in the coal-mines of north-west Durham. The traditional method of coal-getting in this coal-field was *single-place working*. Small groups of miners worked their own place in the coal-seam. They hewed the coal from the face, loaded it into tubs, and propped up the roof as they advanced. Each miner was an all-rounder possessing the necessary skills to carry out all tasks at the face. The groups were self selecting. They were paid according to the amount of coal they hewed *as a group*, and this was shared out equally. The fact that groups were self selecting and each man in them could do all the jobs helped create harmonious relations in them. Relations between groups were also harmonious largely because they did not compete and because they were not subject to detailed management from above. They were capable of organizing the task of getting coal for themselves so long as management provided safe access to the workplace and the necessary services. This pattern of work organization had evolved gradually and was well adapted to the technology of single-place working.

In north-west Durham, the single-place technology was being replaced by mechanized systems of coal-getting. One of these, the *conventional longwall method*, entails strict specialization by shift. One shift undercuts a long wall of coal using a mechanical coal cutter and loosens the rest of the coal by explosive. The next shift loads the loose coal on to a moving conveyer which takes it away from the face. The task for the third shift is to prop up the roof and move the cutter and conveyer up ready for the next cutting and explosive operation. Here we see how a certain kind of work organization has been decided upon as appropriate to a certain kind of technology. The technical means available are the cutter, the explosives and the conveyer. But there is no single answer to the question 'What kind of human organization is best suited to exploit these technical means in such a way as to promote social and psychological satisfaction?' In this case the management had decided that specialization by shift and specialization of role were to be the chief characteristics of work organization. So that each shift, instead of comprising a number of men skilled in all the tasks required to hew and remove coal and keep the workplace safe, comprised men all of whom were skilled at one specialized task. This did not prove successful. Members of shifts were not always able to get along together when it became clear that some were more able and willing than others to perform the task. Further, specialization by shift and role called for co-ordination from outside the work force, to see that each shift completed its bit of the total cycle and to ensure that each member of a shift was doing his fair share of the work and co-operating with others. Whereas in single-place working the groups were self-regulating, they were now closely managed. This, as the researchers point out, is not a suitable organization for work in dangerous situations. A system of working which promotes group cohesion *is* appropriate. The outcome of this form of work organization was technical and economic inefficiency and social and psychological disturbance.

The composite longwall method applies a different form of work organization to the same technology. Here the multi-skilled role is introduced again and specialization minimized. The three-shift cycle obtains, but there is no sharp division of task between shifts. The team as a whole is given and accepts responsibility for the deployment of men to shifts and jobs. This is really duplicating as far as possible within longwall technology the social and psychological conditions of single-place working, i.e. group autonomy, self-regulation and multi-skilled roles. Composite working proves to be conducive to productive efficiency and social and psychological satisfaction.

The practical lesson of *Organizational Choice* is clear. If, as a manager, one has to introduce technical or administrative changes, it is wise first to work out what consequences are likely to follow from adopting one or other of the many organizational alternatives which are possible and then to choose the one which offers the best balance of advantages. This point will be taken up and examined in more detail in Part III. For the moment, we examine some of the problems attending upon the introduction of radical changes in working practices in a British plant as these were reported by Allan Flanders.

THE FAWLEY PRODUCTIVITY AGREEMENTS

It is not usual for managers, particularly perhaps British managers, consciously and consistently to apply a 'philosophy' of industrial relations, in trying to solve administrative problems; at any rate a 'philosophy' which takes account of some of the things social scientists have been saying about organizations and the people who work in them. Nor is it usual for British managers to take the initiative in proposing radical changes in working arrangements which cut across and threaten customary ways, in the certain knowledge that this will give rise to difficulties and in trying to anticipate what these might be. Therefore, an account of what happened when the unusual was attempted is of particular interest for this essay. Allan Flanders[29] describes and analyses the causes and consequences of the 'Blue Book' proposals made by the management of the Fawley Refinery of the Esso Company, having been given access to the facts by the management and by the Unions.

The Fawley refinery was opened in 1951. At the time of its opening it was already destined for a mention in the annals of British industrial relations. The American contractors who built the plant had insisted on negotiating with representatives of the Confederation of Unions instead of with each individual union. The success of this move in smoothing industrial relations was claimed to be a major factor in the speedy and efficient completion of the refinery, and the British Institute of

Management published a short study[30] which described what had happened. By the mid-fifties most of the technical 'bugs' inevitable in a new plant had been successfully dealt with and the refinery was settling down to normal working, but at this time a number of pressures from outside persuaded the management that the efficiency of the refinery ought to be improved. The American parent company, faced with stiff price competition, had taken steps to reduce labour costs by a drastic alteration of working practices and some pruning of manpower. As a result, unfavourable comparisons were made with the situation at Fawley, where no such radical changes had been made. There were those at Fawley who were inclined to use arguments about social structure and cultural differences between Britain and the U.S.A. as an excuse for inaction. But gradually it came to be more widely felt that to allow things to remain unchanged would reflect badly upon the refinery, the British company, and the professional position of the managers themselves. The need for management to take the initiative in this was argued by a small group of managers led by an energetic and knowledgeable senior executive, aided and abetted by a member of an American consulting team called in to investigate working methods. In 1958 the consultant wrote a memorandum proposing that the management should make a sharp attack upon the problem of inefficient utilization of labour. He referred chiefly to excessive overtime. Flanders describes the consultant's proposals as amounting to a high wage/low overtime policy. This was exactly the opposite of the policy which had come to be accepted in the refinery, which was that wages should be about the same as those paid for similar work in the locality but with 'superior' fringe benefits, and that overtime was necessary for technical reasons and also to satisfy the workers.

The means suggested by the consultant for achieving a high wage/ low overtime situation were received with a good deal of scepticism amongst the managers because they seemed blatantly to ignore the obvious obstacles: a complicated and inflexible trade union structure, prevailing strongly held customary interests and beliefs, and entrenched attitudes and practices. It was proposed, for example, to redeploy craftsmen's mates and to upgrade some of them to craftsmen, to amalgamate the various unskilled and semi-skilled grades into one general labouring grade, by a process of attrition to reduce the working force gradually by a third, to cut out travelling and washing time and to introduce a forty-hour week. Impossible as most managers thought

47

this to be, there were some who were inclined to try to work out in detail what the possible consequences of introducing such measures might be, and to begin to test out opinion amongst the men and their unions through the well-developed machinery for consultation which already existed in the plant.

Up to a point the situation compares with that described by Gouldner in the work discussed earlier. Here again was a management faced with inefficient working practices buttressed by a strongly entrenched pattern of customary expectations, of a kind which Gouldner described as the 'indulgency pattern'. But as we move away from that very general comparison to the details, the similarities disappear. At Fawley all the managers were not themselves so closely enmeshed in the customary pattern as to be incapable of co-operating in changes designed radically to disturb it, and a small group of them were eager to make changes but aware of some of the difficulties which faced them. The trade unions were much more strongly represented at Fawley, and the complicated system of collective bargaining, which in Britain goes with such representation in the multi-union plants typical of much of British industry, had no parallel in American plants. There was also the tradition in Britain that in wage negotiations it is usually the unions who take the initiative, and the existing dividing lines between manual occupations, as reflected in union demarcation lines, are inviolate. In short, the management at Fawley had bigger obstacles to overcome but were aware of the size and shape of some of them.

The 'Blue Book', a bulky document, the result of a year's work of drafting, arguing and consulting, amounted to what Flanders has described as a 'productivity package deal'. In the process, the management detailed minutely the measures they proposed to adopt to get more efficient utilization of labour, and set out plainly what they were prepared to offer in return for the abandonment of cherished practices. They were also aware—and Flanders stresses this—of the fact that formal acceptance of the proposals by the unions did not necessarily mean that the men on the plant would find them acceptable, that they would be happy and satisfied with them. The Fawley management did not, like so many British managements, act as if once a collective agreement had been reached with union officials the job of disciplining workers into submission could be left to the unions; as if a promise by a full-time official of a trade union to put an end to a certain restrictive practice necessarily means that it will come to an end. They were aware of the need to generate at shop-floor level a conviction that changes were necessary, and a willingness to accept them in practice. Only in this way, they felt, would they create an atmosphere in which agreements reached around the bargaining table would find their full expression on the job. They also knew that even when this had been done there would still be no automatic acceptance. There would have to be lengthy explanation, protracted discussion, occasionally bitter argument, and they were not surprised when all these things happened. Yet, as Flanders points out, until forced to take notice of it, the management at Fawley overlooked 'the informal structure of organization which is intermediary between the unions and the men as individuals'. Because of this some of the consequences of the Blue Book were unanticipated and disappointing.

The arguments and difficulties which followed during the 1960s from the Blue Book and its successor, the Orange Book, as these are described by Flanders, and the social stresses and tensions generated in the process of change once change had been accepted, demonstrate the inertial force which inheres in social institutions and in the customary expectations and practices which are its expression.

Flanders assesses the results under three headings: economic, institutional and cultural. In economic terms the aim was to raise labour productivity and distribute the gains fairly, without undue increases in cost. Institutionally, the hopes and expectations were that the productivity agreements and their consequences would demonstrate the advantages to be gained by co-operation to improve the refinery as a place of employment, as against the disadvantages of the institutionally enshrined formal haggling over trivia. Culturally, the aim was to generate a different kind of spirit in social relationships in the plant. Flanders concludes that to a considerable measure these three aims were achieved, but argues that to preserve and consolidate the situation needs continual care, attention and hard work, a better understanding of the industrial plant as a social system, and a capacity to learn this by experience.

In a chapter advancing some general conclusions of wider application Flanders draws attention to the fact so often described by social scientists that quite apart from the so-called restrictive practices of trade union agreements, groups of workers will exercise control over their own particular working situation in what they believe to be their own best interests. Indeed, the trade union agreements might well be the outcome of this desire to control for protective reasons. We encountered this phenomenon of group control over output and earnings in our discussion of the Hawthorne investigations. We shall, almost immediately, discuss it in more detail, in the belief that the contribution of the sociologist and social psychologist to the understanding of the behaviour of working groups is of crucial practical importance. But first we must sum up the lessons of the Fawley study.

Flanders argues, persuasively, that managers ought to take the initiative in proposing changes in working practices to improve efficiency, and in working out the implications of such changes for wages, earnings, differentials and so on. They ought not to wait for trade unions to demand more and then find reasons for not meeting fully their demands. And the reason why this must be so is that it cannot, in reason, be shown that the unions have parity with management in managing the workplace. By reason of their technical knowledge and their power position, managers are much better placed than trade union officials to conduct the affairs of the workplace. The role of trade unions is, *inter alia*, to criticize what managers are doing. The attitudes which are generated in the workplace by the interaction between managerial control systems and the control systems by which workers protect themselves from their possible consequences are outside the control of the unions. Yet, Flanders goes on, if this is accepted, there are social and cultural barriers to be overcome. Unless managers understand what these are, unless they have some theoretical understanding of the nature of the system they are working with, either consciously or intuitively, they are likely to fail. We are arguing here exactly the same point.

THE WORKING GROUP AND 'RESTRICTION OF OUTPUT'

We referred earlier to the problem described by Taylor as 'systematic soldiering', i.e. group control over methods of working, levels of output and earnings, to produce output below the expectations of management. From where Taylor stood the obvious practical remedy for this was careful attention to the formal organization of division of labour and the exploitation of individual economic motives, to offset the restrictive influence of the group. As a result of the Bank Wiring Room observations and their other studies, the investigators at Hawthorne had come to a quite different set of conclusions. They said, in effect, that men at work will elaborate their relationships beyond those formally imposed by the necessities of the task in hand; in doing so, they might well develop group standards of behaviour, among which may be a norm of output lower than management expects. They will not do so consciously in pursuit of declared aims, but as a protective reaction to stimuli from the external environment of the group. If the environment is felt to be hostile a group might well control its situation in a restrictive way; if it is benign, the opposite might happen.

On this line of argument, there is no use in trying to break up groups in order to increase the output of individuals. This will merely withdraw much needed social support from the individual, affect morale, and hence performance. As a practical point, if a manager does not understand about groups and if he is faced with 'restriction of output', on balance he might be wise to leave well alone. If he does understand about groups, he will concern himself with the balance of advantages between leaving not-so-well alone, or taking action to create a benign group environment as far as this is within his power, while at the same time giving attention to the organizational changes which need to be made to increase output, and the effect those might have on group structure and cohesion.

From what has been said so far, it should be clear that the need to understand about groups is an essential practical asset to management. In the case of the mechanization of the coal-mines of North West Durham, much inefficiency and dissatisfaction seemed to have been caused by a failure to design working methods in tune with group values. At Fawley, the managers ran up against avoidable difficulties because they failed to take the working group sufficiently into account. Yet, in addition to those already mentioned, there have been many studies of working groups by social scientists, which for all their theoretical differences of emphasis, point very much the same practical lessons. On the whole, these lessons do not seem to have been learned by managers.

It seems so obvious as to be hardly worth repeating that the link between the individual and the large organization is the relationship with a small group of working colleagues, and the same might be said whether the large organization is an industrial firm, a civil service department, a hospital or a university. Yet the implications of this fact are often missed, namely that for the individual there will occur situations of conflict when there is pressure by the organization to behave in ways of which the group disapproves. When this occurs, the individual will respond mostly to the pressure of the group. However, there may arise situations in which doing what is required and valued by the group supports the formal requirements of the organization. It would therefore seem wise to attempt to find out in which circumstances this is likely to happen.

As Dubin[31] has pointed out, the social control systems of small groups (the procedures they adopt for finding out what individuals are doing, and for bringing them into line if what they are doing offends against group norms) are much more effective than the procedures of control devised by the large organization of which the groups form a part. The organization cannot effectively police every individual item of behaviour; the group can, if it wishes. So it would seem wise, if one can create a situation in which the group perceives its environment as benign, to leave the detailed control of individual behaviour to the group; a very different conclusion from the one which Taylor advocated; one which most of the studies reported in this section would in their various ways support. Yet the question of the steps to be taken to create a benign environment for the group still remains an open one, and the influence of technology and other factors in determining the limits of managerial action to control the environment of the group has not yet been fully explored. In the rest of this section some of the questions remaining are discussed by reference to the Bank Wiring Room and to studies carried out by the present writer and some colleagues at Manchester University.[16]

I do not intend to relate in detail the facts observed in the Bank Wiring Room at Hawthorne. These have been reported and discussed extensively elsewhere and the sources are readily available. Under observation, fourteen men engaged upon the wiring-up of terminal 'banks' for telephone exchanges were seen to develop into a fairly cohesive group with cliques inside it, each with special interests and a special role. Certain individuals were also allocated special roles and statuses by the group. The factors determining the structure of the group and the cliques within it seemed to be the layout of the job and the formal organization of the division of labour by management (i.e. factors relating to technology) and the personal characteristics of individuals. The layout and division of labour prescribed the technologically necessary interactions between persons and these in turn led to the development of common sentiments and points of view. Some of these related to the formal organization and division of labour.

Because the control of the minute details of group life by management was necessarily incomplete, there developed group controls in the interstices as it were of the managerial control system. These were turned mainly to the manipulation of the incentive payment system and the level of output. The group set a ceiling on output and maintained it through its control of the system of 'booking' time. So much for the facts. The observers in the Bank Wiring Room interpreted these as meaning that the processes of group formation are not willed deliberately as protective devices or as positive means to serve interests consciously perceived and formulated. Other students of these facts, and of other groups have concluded that there are elements of deliberation in group controls in pursuit of particular interests. Roy, [15] an American student of industrial groups, remarked of one of his groups that they 'made noises like economic men' and this is probably the point of view implicit in Flanders' analysis of informal groups. This difference in emphasis in interpretation has its practical consequences. It is one thing to recognize a rational difference of economic interest expressed in the form of group behaviour, and another to claim that the difference of interest is a non-rational outcome of group processes. Here, I have overstressed the contrast between two points of view in order to show how a theoretical difference may lead to different practical policies.

The similarities between social scientists who have studied working groups are, however, of greater practical importance than the differences. Social scientists are mostly agreed about the factors which shape group structure and behaviour. These are first the technological and administrative arrangements which define necessary relations between roles (and the individual incumbents). However, as Trist[28] and others have pointed out, technology does not impose rigid limits on the organizational forms which might be adopted in any given case. Secondly, there are the personal characteristics of the individual incumbents of the roles. Personal characteristics here refer to the values and beliefs which the individual cherishes, as well as to his mental endowment and qualities of character. If technology (broadly defined) and personal characteristics are the major determinants of group structure and behaviour, then it would follow that group structure and behaviour would tend to differ very much from organization to organization and from department to department within an organization, which is clearly so. These differences stand out sharply in my own comparative study of behaviour in two workshops, one in the electrical engineering industry and one in the garment industry.

In the electrical engineering workshop, which employed men on assembly work, the group had evolved an elaborate system of control over the level of earnings. As in the Bank Wiring Room there was much solidarity in the group as a whole, competing cliques within it, a fairly well-defined informal division of labour within the group related to the task of controlling the payment system and the allocation of work, and a system of subtle social sanctions to control the behaviour of individuals. In the garment workshop, which employed women on assembly, there was much sociability but such social cohesion as there was had not been directed to attempts to control output and earnings. The differences between the two shops may be explained by reference to a range of factors having a differential effect in the two situations, as for example, the state of the market for the product and for labour, the technology, and the effect of these on the structuring of relationships. The system of wage payment and the methods of supervision are also relevant. So are differences in sex, the extra-factory social roles of the workers and other individual characteristics.

These and other studies offer a guide to the things to look for when trying to explain the behaviour of groups. They are also helpful in indicating what might have to be done if group behaviour is to be changed. It is the analytical approach of the social scientist to small group behaviour which offers most help to the practical men of affairs. Large generalizations from small studies of small groups are unhelpful.

The emphasis in this part has been on the analytical method of social science, and particularly sociology, rather than on particular findings of particular studies or experiments. In the final section, a brief account will be given of the present state of theory about organization, which brings in disciplines other than sociology and psychology and explains current controversies. It is hoped, however, that at this point the reader will be ready to follow an attempt in the next section to apply this analytical approach to some selected problems of industrial organization as these are customarily defined by managers. The switch is now from the world of the social scientist to the world of the manager.

III

The Manager's Problems:
What Social Science has to Offer

The Manager's Problems:
What Social Science has to Offer

We are now ready to apply methods and findings of social science to some typical problems of management. First, it is necessary to repeat the warning given earlier that social science is not magic. There are no rabbits to be pulled out of hats. Social science must be seen by managers as a method of analysis and as suggesting courses of action and decision.

Four problems of practical interest to managers will be discussed briefly and some of the concepts previously defined brought to bear upon them. The problems are:

Industrial conflict
Joint consultation and industrial participation
Incentives and motivation
Technical and administrative change.

The treatment of these will be quite brief, the assumption being that the reader will be sufficiently familiar with the language and general approach of social science by now.

INDUSTRIAL CONFLICT

For convenience of analysis, industrial conflict may be treated as being of two kinds. There are firstly those conflicts of interest, opinion and value which interfere with co-operation. Secondly there are complete breakdowns of co-operation such as occur in strikes. In reality, as we shall argue, these are not different in kind, but different ways in which the same conflict manifests itself. We begin with the extreme case—the strike, which is a complete, but temporary, breakdown of co-operative relationships between managers and workers. If we can explain the causes of strikes, we ought to be able to indicate what might be done to avoid them or to limit them, if this is so desired. If strikes are rightly supposed to be an extreme form of non-co-operation, then the explanation of go-slow, work-to-rule, restriction of output and other less violent and obvious forms of conflict will also emerge, and with it possible practical steps to be taken in dealing with them.

Gouldner, in the work previously discussed, traced one set of social processes leading to a strike. He started, as we said, by describing a small industrial unit which exhibited a stable pattern of relationships which was highly valued by all concerned. This 'indulgency pattern', as he called it, appeared to have emerged mainly from the influence of a benign economic environment, reinforced by the effect of kinship and neighbourliness on working relationships in the factory. The resulting customary practices and procedures were highly valued by those concerned with their operation. The 'indulgency pattern' did not give a highly efficient use of economic and technical resources; far from it, but apparently it did give everyone a lot of satisfaction.

The attempt to abolish rapidly some of the satisfaction-giving procedures, to introduce new and more formal technical and administrative ways of doing things and of controlling the things that were done, and to appoint new men in authority to do them, generated resistance. This took the form of sabotage and of attempts to invoke formal machinery of negotiation through trades unions. The sabotage led to counter-measures which included tighter technical and administrative control, closer personal supervision of work and the counter-use of formal machinery. The progressive break-up of the 'indulgency pattern' was now well under way and this process became practically irreversible. More control bred more tension; adaptation took the form of counter-controls, which were countered by more formal controls, which bred more tension and more sabotage. In the absence of well-developed and subtly designed mechanisms for the redress of grievance, a complete breakdown of relationships was the inevitable result—the 'wildcat strike' Gouldner describes. Once co-operation had broken down completely, a new process had to start to generate an atmosphere in which co-operative relations could be resumed and social mechanisms established for the redress of future grievances.

If one were to hazard a generalization at this stage it would be that attempts at radical administrative or technical change, without regard to the provision of social mechanisms for dealing with their consequences, bid fair to end in social breakdown. What these social mechanisms are and how they may be introduced is left for later discussion. However, some things stand out clearly from Gouldner's analysis of the Gypsum factory case and from many other studies. One of these is that the attempt to design a new management structure and new working practices and to introduce them as if they only had to be explained to be acceptable is likely to fail. Paradoxically, although such attempts might seem rational means to economic ends supposedly desired by everybody, they might well set in motion social processes leading to a complete breakdown of co-operation.

In the case described by Gouldner it was the introduction of formal administrative procedures of control which started the process. But we saw, when we considered the work of Joan Woodward and of the Liverpool University team, that the nature of the production technology might have an effect on role expectations and on the way in which technological change is assimilated. So we must not say that strikes or other forms of non-co-operation will necessarily follow technical and administrative change. If, for example, the technology is such as to afford some intrinsic satisfaction in the job, if there are well-developed formal methods of joint negotiation and dispute procedure, if there is time to use the machinery, and if the general social and economic environment is such as to encourage goodwill, then people may well co-operate in the process of change. In the steelworks studied by the Liverpool team, the situation had many of these features.

It is useful to describe what we have been discussing as *structural conflict*. A manager contemplating changes in the way his company or department is administered, or the engineer planning a new layout or the use of new machinery, or an organization and methods man thinking about new procedures for control, would be wise to ask two questions: first, what is the likely effect on roles, expectations, the social structure of the situation generally; second, are the procedures which already exist for dealing with change capable of handling such difficulties as seem likely to arise?

Before going on to discuss another type of conflict-generating situation, it is necessary to deal with a possible objection to the argument so far. What about human malice, stupidity, irrationality? What about agitators, and people who are so daft that they cannot see where their own best interests lie? Is not this kind of thing the cause of most of the troubles of management? Do we need all this stuff about role expectations and social structure? Take agitators first. Social scientists are not the only people who think systematically about social situations. If a person has an intuitive grasp of the fact that processes which threaten eventual social breakdown have been induced, and he is convinced that this is a good thing because it will embarrass his enemies, then if he is able to do so he will take steps, more or less skilfully, to hasten the process. Naturally, he will come up against those who do not want the process to go on, and name-calling ensues. The name-calling is an effect, not a cause. As for daft people who cannot see where their own best interests lie, it would seem that persons and groups come to define their own best interests from their shared social experience. They do not on the whole take kindly to statements from others that if they took this or that factor into account, they would soon see that they were mistaken. They might, however, change if their social experience changed.

Straight conflicts of economic interest, which we distinguish from structural conflicts, are the result of a deliberate decision to coerce employers in one way or another to part with more cash or power, or to give better working conditions. It is not being suggested here that strikes are *either* the result of tensions arising from frustrated role-expectations *or* of decisions to try open coercion when other means have failed. Both elements are likely to be present in any strike. What *is* being suggested is that there are conflicts about pay. There are also procedures for bargaining about pay, and for avoiding a breakdown of co-operation emerging from failure to agree, and there are fairly rational means for dealing with conflicts of interest. Sometimes, the machinery proves incapable of handling the demands made upon it and open coercion is employed. As every student of collective bargaining knows, the hidden sanction of strike or lockout always underlies bargaining. But usually industrial conflict is both a structural conflict and an interest conflict; indeed, it is only possible to separate the two analytically, never in practice.

When we discussed Flanders' study of changes in working practices at Fawley we saw how problems arose from the formal clash of interests over pay and conditions with trade union officials, and how the managers tried to anticipate, with some success, the social structural effects of change on the attitudes of the workers themselves. If the managers had not done so, if they had seen the only problem of administrative change as the negotiation of new wage rates, new job definitions, and so on through the formal machinery, they might possibly have set in train the circular process of structural tension, sabotage, tight control, tension, sabotage, etc. But they tried not only to anticipate the structural effects of the changes they were proposing. They also tried to prepare people for these changes. The same kind of procedure was adopted by the managers in the Liverpool steelworks study. What is being done here, in effect, is to create a special temporary structure of role relationships for preparing for, and handling the consequences of, structural change. It was the absence of awareness of the need for this machinery of social transition, and of opportunities to create it, which was part of the difficulty in the Gypsum factory.

The practical lessons of all this are quite clear. Firstly, managers ought not to rely too heavily on formal machinery for settling conflicts of economic interest in conditions of social and administrative change. At least, they ought to examine this machinery to see if it seems adequate to handle the structural consequences of change. They ought also to consider seriously what additional social mechanisms can be created to ease the transition. Later, in a discussion of Joint Consultation, we will be discussing this point more fully.

A third kind of conflict which we have to discuss is that arising from dissatisfaction with the job itself. It has been argued persuasively from empirical evidence that good environmental conditions—so called 'job hygiene', i.e. good welfare facilities, meals, lighting, heating, good mates—are not as important in promoting satisfaction in work as the actual job itself. Yet, it is often economically and technologically necessary, as in the situation described by Walker and Guest, so to divide the total task in pursuit of productive efficiency that each individual job offers little or no satisfaction. If we assume that people expect their jobs to give them satisfaction, then we should also expect that to do unsatisfying work day in and day out might lead to protest. The protest could take the form of an individual decision to leave and get another job. It could take the form of attempts, either by individuals or groups, to provide in the job situation some compensating satisfactions, such as pitting wits against management on piecework rates. Or it could take the form of periodic stoppages of work. It is difficult to say, because this would depend upon circumstances, just what form the protest might take, but (again assuming that people expect to get satisfaction from their jobs) a manager might well anticipate some kind of protest in reaction. This element of job dissatisfaction might enter also into structural conflict. The tension generated by frustrated social expectations might be heightened by 'fed-upness' with the job itself. All this suggests that it would be unwise for a manager to rely too much on the effects of welfare facilities, or even high wages, to offset the frustrating effects of unsatisfying jobs. To allow scope for workers to develop their own compensating mechanisms might be much better. It is possible that, in general, industrial workers do not expect their jobs to be satisfying, but regard the hours spent at work as unpleasant interludes yielding income which enables them to seek satisfaction elsewhere.

There is some evidence—which would tell against this line of argument—that restrictive practices, which are a form of restricted co-operation, arise from attempts by workers to do two things: first to protect their long-term sectional economic interests and, second, to compensate for the unsatisfactory nature of the work, or the uncertainties in management planning, by individual or group control over the work. The practical solution to this problem is difficult. To attempt root and branch administrative reform might promote structural conflict, conflict of economic interest and dissatisfaction with the job and the relationships involved in it. The task of the manager is to think out a line of action which offers scope for job satisfaction, and/or scope for compensating control, and which at the same time leads to technical and administrative efficiency. This sounds very difficult, and rather than attempt it many managers would argue that it is sufficient to provide a forum where men can air their grievances and management can inform them of what it proposes to do, and to try in general to promote a sense of loyalty to the company and a feeling of mutual interest. Some of the practical shortcomings of the 'sense of belonging and mutual interest' approach will have become apparent by now. In the next short section we discuss them in more detail.

To sum up, industrial conflict is the likely outcome of attempts to organize co-operation in situations of technical and economic complexity. It can manifest itself as structural conflict; conflict for scarce resources of cash and the power to influence events; or conflict arising from protest against boring, monotonous work. Actual conflict may well emerge as a mixture of the three, when an organization is confronted with the need to change its technology or its administrative procedures. Some industries seem more prone to conflict of all three kinds than others. There is evidence that mining and dock work, wherever in the world one finds them, are conflict-prone. Other industries, such as textiles, seem less so. This is probably because the environment in which strife-ridden industries are living is less benign. The economics of dock work, prey to tides, weather, and the vagaries of world shipping, combined with geographic isolation which promotes cohesion amongst a casual labour force, go far to explaining the high incidence of conflict. They do not go all the way. Examples of a low incidence of conflict in an industry normally conflict-prone can be found, the outcome of successful attempts to overcome the disadvantages of the environment. It is also possible for managers and workers to develop ill will when all the external circumstances are favourable to goodwill and co-operation. Yet, the opportunities obviously differ greatly, and it is clear that some managers who want to limit, guide and control the level of conflict will encounter more difficulties than others. The social scientist is able to point out the likely result of certain external conditions, such as location, technology, labour markets and product markets, in creating the conditions for conflict. With this knowledge the manager may take the measure of his problems and begin to estimate the likely success of this or that change in policy.

JOINT CONSULTATION AND INDUSTRIAL PARTICIPATION

The term Joint Consultation is usually used to describe the formal machinery through which the managers and the workers in a firm, or their elected or appointed representatives, discuss their common problems, decide about them and exchange information. In some firms there is no such formal machinery. Where it does exist, it differs much from firm to firm. And in the majority of cases a sharp distinction is drawn between the machinery of Joint Consultation and the machinery of collective bargaining. This section is not intended to be a detailed description of the practice of Joint Consultation and it will examine the question of worker participation in decision-making and management in a much wider context. It might be useful, however, before looking at Joint Consultation and participation in the light of social science findings, to describe a typical example.

In a small firm, Joint Consultation might take place in a Works Committee, composed of elected or appointed workers representing departments, and managers nominated by the chief executive or serving in rotation. The worker representatives may or may not be union shop stewards, depending on whether the union is strong, and on its views about Joint Consultation. In a large firm there may be departmental committees dealing with local matters and sending agenda items and representatives forward to a larger committee at works level. The agenda of all committees will usually exclude topics considered by the trades unions to be matters for the collective bargaining machinery. The items remaining could well include the consideration of productivity figures and proposals for improvement, welfare services and canteens, the administration of a profit-sharing scheme, or exchanging information about the firm's position and problems. Rarely would they lead to decisions encroaching on managerial prerogatives.

In its most common expression, the theory of Joint Consultation comprises a few straightforward propositions about human nature and industrial organization. It is held, firstly, that individuals feel better if they are given an opportunity, either directly or indirectly, at the most to participate in those decisions which affect their jobs and hence their living, at the least to be informed of what decisions have been taken and why. The second hypothesis is that an organization wishing to keep its employees satisfied should provide a forum where they can voice their minor grievances and canvass ideas for improvement. Thirdly, while it might be admitted that there are issues and occasions for conflict in industry, there are also many more points of common interest and objective between managers and workers than are normally explicit in the day-to-day business of getting the job done, and Joint Consultation helps to provide the means to seek common ground. Fourthly, there are many matters of administration; of sports clubs, bonus and profit-sharing schemes and the like, where the organizing talents of the ordinary employee can find opportunities denied to him unavoidably in everyday work. Fifthly, it is usually supposed that if the facilities for participation and the forum for discussion are provided the employees will feel better about working for the firm. The result then will be lower turnover and absence rates, a lower incidence of conflict, a feeling of loyalty and belonging, and in all probability a greater will to work. Finally, Joint Consultation allows managers and workers to meet in circumstances where their relationship of subordinate to superior is played down, and their common role as employees of the firm, equally concerned with its fortunes, is played up, and this, it is claimed, is good for everyone's morale.

One can cite examples where a formal system of committees, designed to give effect to these theories and taken seriously by the management of the firm, has worked in the sense that it has engaged the interest of the employees at least to the point where they are prepared to vote, to stand for elections, and in general to become in some way involved. But it is difficult to measure exactly the effect of such a system. It is easy therefore for the sceptic to point to the impossibility of isolating the effect of Joint Consultation from all the other effects on relationships within the firm, or to argue that perhaps the apparent success of Joint Consultation is the effect and not the cause of harmonious relationships. It is possible to cite even more examples where Joint Consultation systems were set up only to fall speedily into disuse for lack of interest or of things to discuss, and even more where the committees carry on as management tribunals for the periodic hearing of the minor grievances of the shop floor and the announcement of management intentions. To refer back to the theory does not help explain the successes, the failures or the scepticism. Is there anything in social science which does?

We had better refer, in answer to that question, to what social scientists have to say about the causes and consequences of employee participation, to find out whether there is anything there which would support the common-sense theory previously summarized, and if there is what it implies for practical policy. We had also better ask whether social scientists have any way in which they can measure the effect of adopting or not adopting this or that system of joint consultation or employee participation. However, before we do this we might as well say that the simple practical reason why Joint Consultation is often introduced is a belief that the industrial firm should practise some form of democracy. Since no great harm is likely to ensue from the attempt to do so, it is easy to indulge in it, and it is unimportant whether it exists alongside high labour turnover, unofficial strikes and the like, which occur, it is believed, for reasons other than the presence or absence of democracy.

Probably the most serious practical attempt to explore the relationship between industrial efficiency and industrial democracy and to devise means to combine them has taken place at the Glacier Metal Company in London. It would take up much more space than I have at my disposal to describe this exploration in detail, but the main outlines of the theory and practice are clear. At Glacier they subscribe up to a point to the theories of formal organization which we discussed earlier. They argue the value of clarity of role definition and role relationships, and the importance of avoiding confusion arising from conflicting definitions of the same activity (for example, what management is), and aim to clear away misunderstanding about words and symbols. They have sought to devise efficient formal systems of authority, responsibility and function, and patterns of communication, and to seek for equitable ways of deciding differential rewards for work done. All this has been done carefully and systematically, using concepts derived from the social sciences. In pursuit of efficiency they have tried to build a stable structure of formal role expectations, which embodies importantly a written code of rules governing behaviour and relationships. The social analysts at Glacier Metal were interested in the question which Gouldner raised, namely, who makes the rules in bureaucracies and what effect this knowledge has on the attitudes of employees.

After a good deal of detailed action research* on the working of orthodox Joint Consultation in situations where rule-making was almost entirely a management prerogative, it came to be believed that relationships in the firm would become much more harmonious and effective if the making of rules governing behaviour were jointly done by committees representing all grades and skills—a legislative system— and if once the rules were made the management were entirely responsible to the legislators for administering them effectively—the executive system. The attempt has been made, and the experiments are still going on, to extend this system of democratic management throughout the company, in such a way that the autonomy of small units within the company to decide and act is pushed as far as is consistent with overall co-ordination and the use of specialist services. The merits claimed for this system are that it allows free play to the desire of men to participate, however humbly, in matters affecting their work; it provides channels through which people can learn quickly the consequences of decisions and take appropriate action; it affirms managerial authority and it creates an atmosphere where people feel free to express themselves knowing that redress against arbitrary authority is to be had. In all, it removes some of the inequalities and injustices which generate tension, uneasiness and distrust, making it possible for people to work effectively in roles which are clearly defined and equitably rewarded.

Here, at Glacier Metal, is an example of a collaboration of a rather unusual kind between social scientists and managers over many years. Workers and managers have been involved in a continuous process of analysis of the organization and many changes have come about as a result. The outcome of this collaboration [32, 33, 34] deserves the attention of all practising managers and social scientists. There is, however,

---

*Research which is directed towards the practical improvement of the situation under observation.

a danger that the uncritical propagation of the Glacier 'system' as a general set of principles of management might lead to exact imitation in situations where it is inappropriate, or where the personal skills required by managers are lacking. There is also a danger that the underlying value premise of the Glacier work will be uncritically accepted, namely that it is part of the responsibility of industrial managers to promote industrial harmony, to play down conflict and tensions, on the ground (a) that to do so leads to industrial efficiency and (b) that it promotes emotional security and a sense of belonging, and that both of these are good. Another equally valid but contrasting premise might be that the task of management is to allow considerable free play to individual and sectional interests and to set up machinery for avoiding the worst consequences of the rational pursuit of sectional self-interest. The basic assumption in this case would be that managers ought to manage according to rules which serve their interests, and workers ought to have scope to resist those consequences of management which affect their interests.

In an important sense the Glacier Metal project is in the Hawthorne tradition, in taking the view that the task of management is not just a technical one. It is also a job of creating a social organism in which everyone can participate to the greatest possible degree and with which everyone can feel a sense of close identification. Also in the tradition of the Hawthorne experiments stand Likert[35] and his colleagues at the University of Michigan, McGregor[36] at the Massachusetts Institute of Technology, and Argyris[37] of Yale. They are in the tradition in the sense that they are interested primarily in finding out which patterns of management and supervision will lead, in general, to (a) the satisfaction of the employee with his lot in the organization, (b) the opportunity for the employee to use his capabilities to the full, (c) the canalization of emotional energy in the direction of the objectives of the organization, and (d) the attainment of productive efficiency.

A short summary will obviously not do justice to the work and ideas of these men, but will suffice in this context. In general, these American writers seem to be saying that, as a result of their own researches and those of other people, it is becoming obvious that the theory of organizational design and managerial control propagated by Taylor, when put into practice, leads to unwanted results. First, it leads to a division of labour which casts many individuals in roles which offer no scope for their talents. These roles cramp and constrain the individual and promote dissatisfaction. Attempts by individuals to compensate for this may take the form, on the workers' side, of restriction of output and other means to control their circumstances so that they *do* offer opportunity to exercise talents and pursue interests. In terms of the theory of formal organization and control this calls for counter managerial control procedures which will reduce the scope for workers' control. But this, by definition, will only increase dissatisfaction further. To attempt to allay dissatisfaction and buy loyalty and co-operation by welfare schemes, fringe benefits and other such inducements will probably have the effect of producing a dead level of apathy about the job, the firm and the management. Restriction of output and sabotage is at least a lively and positive reaction. Formal joint consultation, as it was described at the beginning of this section, would probably be regarded by the writers we are discussing as another attempt to produce *erzatz* identification, while maintaining an authoritarian system of management. The Glacier Metal system would not, of course, be included in this adverse judgement. Secondly, they are saying that it is a legitimate expectation of workers, fostered by a democratic political system and emphasized in modern systems of education, to be given a fair share of the power to influence events. In industrial organization, power equalization has been pushed a long way by the growth of strong trade unions, but this might not mean much to the man on the job in his day-to-day relations with the management. To him the union is a remote thing. Therefore industrial organizations must look for ways and means of meeting this expectation on the job.

As it happens, the research on the consequences of the various styles of management and supervision referred to by these writers seems to point to the welcome fact that democratic forms of management give better results in production efficiency. The researchers have also devised methods of measuring with some accuracy the ways in which members of organizations are influencing decisions in them, the consequences of this upon their attitudes and beliefs and the results of certain patterns of influence on performance. Now, it would appear, we are entitled to more than a vague belief that democratic leadership is good for efficiency. It is strongly claimed that the facts prove it. Democratic leadership can now be more precisely defined and its consequences more precisely measured. If participative and democratic management are really introduced then an improvement in morale and in efficiency will probably follow. As it also happens, there is scope within every production technology for 'job enlargement'. It is not always necessary for production efficiency to make a minute breakdown of the total task so that the skill left in each job is minimal. More often than not the task can be divided in such a way as to make the individual jobs a challenge to skill and ingenuity. Where this is not possible, men can be trained to do more than one job, and can rotate from job to job. It is argued that any inefficiencies arising from job rotation and job enlargement, and there are not likely to be many, will be more than made up by a more positive attitude.

The theorists of participative management, it must again be stressed, are not armchair speculators. Their prescriptions are founded on an impressive body of empirical research, conducted mainly in the U.S.A. By implication they are not very complimentary about formal systems of Joint Consultation with their emphasis on committees and their discussions of welfare. Formal systems offer too easy an excuse for avoiding the main problem, which is how so to manage the technology and administration of production that it offers as an integral part work which exploits individual ability, and which creates for individuals opportunities to take part meaningfully in decisions about important technical and administrative questions.

There is a plausibility about the theories of participative management we have discussed which is difficult to counter, and the underlying democratic value premise is so attractive that it might seem churlish to be critical. There are, however, a number of criticisms to be offered. In the first place, by no means all social scientists are convinced that the research results which are used to back up the theory of participation are as conclusive as they seem, both as regards technical design and in the relation between the data and the conclusions. Secondly, there is a concealed assumption in most of the work that industrial workers want to participate in a positive way and will get satisfaction from it. There is some evidence to the contrary, namely, that some of them prefer to let managers take the decisions, reserving the right to challenge the consequences of these decisions in so far as they affect pay and conditions. Workers, it is said, are very interested in power equalization as it is expressed on economic questions through trade unions in bargaining with management, but not in decisions about production at plant level. Thirdly, the cultural, economic and technical circumstances in which industrial production is carried on have an effect on attitudes towards participation and power equalization. There can be no general prescription for every patient, and certainly there is not complete agreement amongst the prognosticators about the nature of the complaint. Yet social science research has raised new questions about the nature and consequences of Joint Consultation and industrial participation, and has attempted to separate out fact and value in trying to answer them.

INCENTIVE AND MOTIVATION

The ideas of Joint Consultation and of democratic participation of workers in management which we have just been discussing may also be seen as ideas about incentive and motivation. They explain how to structure situations so that the people in them will be moved to behave co-operatively. Metaphorically, they show how to breathe life into formal structures designed to achieve particular objectives. But there are other kinds of incentive, which are much better known and much more frequently resorted to by managers as a means to higher outputs by workers. I refer, of course, to cash incentives.

When in Part I we examined the work of Frederick Taylor, we argued that 'scientific management' rests on a belief that managers and workers have an underlying mutual interest in co-operating effectively with each other. It is only because of lack of forethought by managers that this mutual interest is obscured. According to the tenets of scientific management, the recognition of mutual interest is achieved by a division of labour between managers and operatives in which managers do the planning and organizing and operators do the operating. The responsibility of management, so the argument goes, is to manage, which means to make the best possible use of the resources at its disposal to achieve the objectives set. Operators have an interest in efficient management because it can create more wealth to share out than inefficient management. This interest can never be a direct one because it is inefficient to have operators, who are not trained to plan, to organize and to co-ordinate, interfering with these proper concerns of management. Therefore it is part of the task of management, which it has an obligation to perform efficiently, to define for the operator exactly what is expected of him, and to provide him with the equipment and services necessary to meet these expectations. If the operator is properly selected and trained for the task, then the result of the division of labour between the organizers and the doers ought to result in high outputs, and this makes it possible to give high rewards for the performance of the task.

It is this relation between a clearly defined task and a clearly defined and (notionally) equitable reward for performing it which brings home directly to the operator that he has a vested interest in the prosperity of the firm just as much as managers have. This kind of relationship between effort and cash reward is best described as *task work*.

Task work specifies a relation between the whole task and the whole reward. More conventional schemes of wage payment make greater use of the cash motive, because, unlike task work, they leave some discretion to the operator to produce more bits of work for more pay, or less for less pay, the assumption being that the operator, interested as he is believed to be in making more money ('after all, that's what people come to work for, don't they?') will be moved to make it by producing more output. This is presumed to serve the manager's best interest, too, because he is getting more total output from the factory. So, whether the system of payment is a simple one which offers so much per piece, or a complicated one which includes rewards for quality, machine utilization and so on, the assumption is that the motive of cash reward is sufficient to move the operator to use the discretion given to him in directions desired by management towards higher outputs of high-quality parts. It is also expected that, if the managers do not provide the proper tools and services to make possible the high earnings which the scheme promises, then the frustration of the worker at having to forgo the promised extra cash will lead him to put pressure upon the management to improve these tools and services. Therefore, in an indirect way, the cash motive of workers operating through a payment-by-results scheme can, it is said, keep continual pressure on management to improve.

The theory of task work and the theory of payment-by-results, while different in their application are basically similar in according primacy to cash as a prime mover and in either neglecting or underestimating other motives. They also stress the directness of the relation of payment to results. The individual or the group (if the incentive is a group incentive) ought to see very quickly the reward for effort; otherwise the pulling power of extra cash is weakened.

One approach to a critique of the theory of payment-by-results is to ask what it is which is supposed to motivate managers. In most cases it is impossible clearly to define the task of the manager as a set of separable physical movements or clerical routines. In fact the skill of the manager is very largely a matter of solving non-routine, sometimes quite novel problems, in non-routine and novel ways. It is very difficult to break down his job into measured bits and to pay for the bits; and the total task is not easy to define or to relate to the salary. Yet managers are assumed to have, and the evidence is that they generally do have, a strong motive to do their jobs well and efficiently. They are expected to have an interest in the success of the organization as a whole and to see their job as a contribution; to a much greater extent than the operator, they do so. Managers will, of course, have ideas as to whether the money reward they receive is or is not an equitable reward for what they do, but it is not assumed that they will therefore do work exactly to correspond with the salary and no more. People behave in fact as if they can rely on managers to throw in their lot, as it were, with the organization. Managers will be moved, it is expected, to seek promotion and to work hard for it. Of course, firms pay cash bonuses to their managers, but these are seen as being due to the success of the organization as a whole to which all have contributed and not as a differential reward for a particular bit of effort. And bonuses usually come for managers after the effort has been put in and not as a result of a promise that they will be paid if certain defined tasks are satisfactorily carried out in a given time.

Perhaps an important motive of the manager is a general sense of obligation to the company he works for to do the best he can. In so far as the company prospers he will expect to share in that prosperity and to that extent cash is a strong motive. Yet whether his job be one of providing technical expertise or service, or taking part in making important decisions, or generally co-ordinating and facilitating the work of other men, it is likely to hold an absorbing interest for him.

What then is assumed to be the difference between a worker and a manager? Is it impossible that the worker will be unmoved by loyalty to the company, or that he can never be expected to see that his own prosperity is related to the prosperity of the company, unless this relationship is administratively transmuted into a direct and immediate equation which taps the acquisitive instinct? Is it also assumed that his job will inevitably be so unsatisfying in itself that the only way to overcome natural aversion is a bribe? Advocates of profit-sharing and the various schemes which relate the economic rewards of everyone to the economic success of the company would answer 'No'. They would judge that the worker like the manager could be moved to his best efforts by a sense of obligation to the company that employs him, and that this would be encouraged by the feeling that he was sharing in an economic prosperity (and also perhaps a good name) which he had helped to shape.

Do any of the methods of analysis and findings of social science help illuminate the very practical problems of deciding what kind of wage payment system is the appropriate one for maximizing efficiency and the satisfaction of human motives at work? In the first place, a knowledge of the social science of organizations would lead one to expect in most organizations an uneven formal distribution of the power to influence events; or at least stringent limitations on the extent to which power can be shared out without affecting organizational efficiency. One would also be led to expect attempts to equalize power, the push coming from those who are deprived of it. Power in this context means access to scarce satisfactions of all kinds, monetary and otherwise. The social scientist would also expect that the division of labour in an organization would give rise to groups whose interests and points of view conflict. Power is sought and used partly to pursue those interests.

Within this context, individuals seeking the satisfaction of their material needs and their needs to be well regarded by their fellows and to have satisfactory relationships with them, will try to influence their situation so that it provides these satisfactions. For the worker, whose individual discretion is by definition limited, but who works often in a group, the small group is the vehicle through which he seeks to influence his situation. The group itself may derive some of its power from, say, trade union backing, but it will use this in the context of the small group. Any attempt to exploit one motive, such as the money motive, and to frustrate others will lead to attempts to find other forms of expressing them. This, as we recall, goes some way to explain 'restriction of output'. It also warns us that if a group is restricting output and it is thought necessary to stop it from doing so, it would not be enough merely to find another system of wage payment and put it in, on the assumption that the restriction must be necessarily caused by a fault in the design or administration of the incentive scheme. It might even lead us to ask whether it would be best to leave the group restricting output, since it would appear that unaided they have found ways to satisfy their needs by using their power to control the job, which management had not built into the formal organization. Social science would also lead us to make better guesses at what the outcome would be if it were decided to make changes. We would expect the accretion of custom and informal structure, which, when disturbed, would perhaps generate frustration and tension.

Social science would also suggest that there are limits to an individual's capacity to identify with a large organization. There is much evidence that the behaviour of the individual is controlled more effectively by his fellows in the small group in which he works than by the formal rules and obligations of a large organization. It is true that the organization influences individual behaviour by working through interpersonal influence, but this is much more likely to be effective in a small organization than in a large one comprising many interlinked and interlocking sub and sub-sub units. Social science, therefore, helps us to judge the circumstances which limit the effectiveness of profit-sharing and such-like schemes.

Recently, resulting from a failure in many industries for payment-by-results to meet expectations, and because payment-by-results seems to be a factor promoting the increasing and inflationary tendency for earnings to run far ahead of nationally negotiated wage rates, task work has come again into favour, this time in the guise of *measured* or *controlled daywork*. However, in this new form the earnings are not paid in relation to each separate task performed. Rather a regular weekly wage is guaranteed and this is paid regardless of the number and type of jobs done in the week, as long as on each job the standard of performance agreed between the men and their union and the management is consistently met. Methods such as this, demand a detailed spelling out of a contract between the worker and his boss. The advocates of such schemes argue that the motive being tapped here is the sense of moral obligation to keep contracts into which both parties have voluntarily entered, and which they say is a very strong motive. They also point out that such schemes throw the onus fairly and squarely on management and supervision to manage the process efficiently and to devise the structures of management, supervision and control needed to administer the contract.

Men's motives for working co-operatively with other men are complex and the situations in which they work are complex. Situations differ from organization to organization and from time to time in the same organization. Therefore, it is impossible to give a general answer about the organizational arrangements best fitted to tap men's motives to co-operate. But social science offers means to diagnose each situation so that the alternatives for action are thrown up, and it might well indicate which alternative to adopt. The range of human needs can be defined, and it can be asked whether the present working arrangement, system of wage payment and type of job, are contributing to these needs or not. It can also be asked to what extent those needs are being met by formal organization, to what extent they are being met informally and at what cost to the organization. If the answers prove unsatisfactory, then one must search for alternatives which offer a balance between low cost and high social and individual satisfaction. It might be that any one of the methods we have described for tapping motives, or any combination of them, may give satisfactory results in productivity and job satisfaction in a particular situation. The decision to adopt particular methods or not is a manager's job.

TECHNICAL AND ADMINISTRATIVE CHANGE

Decisions to install new and labour-saving machinery, or to introduce new administrative systems of paper flow, or to add to existing plant, or to improve stockholding facilities, or to introduce a new incentive scheme, all involve a more or less complicated calculation of costs to be incurred against economic benefits to be gained. In the next section we shall refer briefly to the methods which economists have developed for improving the way these calculations are made. For the moment we confine ourself to the social and psychological consequences of the decisions.

It ought to be obvious that social and psychological reactions to the consequences of an economic decision could well give rise to costs which would make the project impractical. It seems often to be assumed that because, in the nature of things, these social and psychological reactions and their costs cannot be measured, they can safely be ignored, or roughly guessed at. There are, in practice, three possible attitudes on the part of managers. *Firstly*, over-confidence that the benefits to be gained so outweigh the costs to be incurred that any cost outcome arising from social resistance will be easily covered; an example of this is the company which introduced a complicated incentive bonus scheme throughout its factory. Convinced that great gains in productivity would accrue, it gave generous pay guarantees to the trade unions in return for their co-operation. Shop-floor sabotage, additional costs of administration to counter the sabotage, and the cost of the guarantee wiped out the anticipated net advantage. *Secondly*, lack of awareness that there could possibly be any social costs. This might arise from taking a crude view that formal organization and money incentives properly organized will make mutual interest obvious. All that is needed then is a calculation of the costs of buying machinery, installing it, putting in an administrative system, and offering money rewards to employees for co-operation. The difficulty here might arise from delays in getting the machinery installed while arguments rage about who is to be transferred, and to which new job, and at what wages. In this case some of the costs have been anticipated; but not the cost of delay. The belief that formal planning would eliminate it makes anticipation unnecessary. *Thirdly*, because of lack of a means to anticipate the difficulties likely to arise, these difficulties are overestimated by management and the project is abandoned. In what way can the methods of social science help in anticipating the social and psychological consequences of technical and administrative innovation?

From what has been said so far we would expect that decisions to innovate would arise in response to a stimulus from the environment of the firm. The situation might call for the development of a new product, or an increase in the output of an old product, or a reduction in the cost of the product. This development in turn suggests technological or administrative improvements. The choice between the alternative technical and administrative means available will usually be made on economic grounds, and one factor in the calculation will obviously be the estimated time available to search for, and to examine the feasibility of, all possible alternatives, and this puts a restriction on the number of alternatives considered. Once the decision is taken, it should then be possible to start a similar search for organizational alternatives, and it is in considering these alternatives that some of the ideas we have been discussing come in useful.

We know that there is some relation between technology and the structure of organizations, and that if technology changes, the structure of the organization will most probably have to change, if the technology is to be efficiently exploited. But we also know that there is no exact correlation between technology and social structure and that for any technology, or for that matter any administrative procedure, there may be a number of organizational alternatives. Our reference to the work of Tom Burns earlier also gave us the idea that mechanistic, rigidly defined structures were not likely to be effective in conditions of innovation. When we looked at the properties of social structure we learned to expect that the accretion of routine and custom which accompanies the development of social structures based on one technology, may obstruct the introduction of another. This inertia, it seems, is probably greater at the points where roles are highly programmed, and where this is accompanied by a high degree of social cohesion, usually at the bottom of the hierarchy. Finally, the inertia might be strengthened by external support for existing custom and practice through trade union demarcation rules. Looking at the organization with these ideas in mind will show not only what organizational alternatives are possible but which of these will lead to the speediest and smoothest assimilation of the innovation. But more of this presently. Now we need to be reminded of what is meant by an 'organizational alternative'.

Trist and his colleagues in their study[28] of mechanization in coal-mines emphasized the general idea that although structural alternatives are limited by technology, they are by no means uniquely determined by technology. That is to say, there is scope for managers to discover what alternatives exist and to choose between them. In the coal-mining example, there appeared to be a number of ways in which the total task of mechanized coal-getting could be divided up between teams on shifts and between the members of the teams. It also seemed possible to specify a number of ways of supervising and servicing the production processes. Such evidence as we have, suggests that the same would apply to any task. For example, the division of labour and the supervisory structure for an electric arc steel furnace, or a steel rolling mill, are not uniquely determined by the design of the machine. Nor does the design of a set of documents and a filing procedure completely limit how an office will be laid out and how the jobs in it will be defined, although it sets some limits. The idea of organizational choice is a great mental stimulus. It abjures technological determinism and raises the question 'If we have a choice, what are the criteria to be used in making it?' If the answer is that the criteria are satisfaction on economic, technical and social and psychological grounds, then just as each technical alternative was judged on its technical and economic merits, so each organizational alternative must be judged on its social and economic merits. Is it the most effective way to exploit the technical advantages of a process? Will it take a lot or a little item to introduce? What social and psychological resistance will it generate? What will be the long-term effects of this? We are now ready to seek methods of organizational diagnosis which will answer some of these questions.

Assume that a decision to innovate has been made and suppose also that several alternative methods of organization have been proposed. How are the likely consequences of adopting one or other of them to be judged? Knowledge of social science is useful in searching for answers. We know that each alternative is going to involve changes in role definition and in role relationships, and these are capable of specification. Then the question can be asked what groupings and individuals are going to be affected, and in what ways, and how are they likely to feel and to reason about it. To approach the same problem from a slightly different angle, we could say that our proposals for organization are directed to a re-structuring of the social and technical environments of groups and individuals. The reactions of these people to this re-structuring will be influenced very much by how much their interests, their expectations, their routines and their customs are going to be affected, much more on the basis of their personal circumstances than on consideration of what the change contributes to the organization as a whole. To estimate the impact of change it is necessary to know what is going to happen to groups and individuals, and what they are likely to do as a consequence. Change cannot be managed intelligently if one has only hazy knowledge and works with an assumption that people and groups will share the interests, routine and customs of all other people and groups and will react in the same way. Nor is it helpful to condemn them if they do not.

There are limits to the extent that any one group in an organization can have intimate knowledge of the expectations, interests, etc., of another, but this should not prevent the attempt to acquire such knowledge and to do so systematically. The formal and informal ways in which conflicts of interest and perspective are usually handled in the organization can also be discovered by careful investigation. We are arguing here for a diagnostic description of the organization as a system in equilibrium. We want to use this to predict the consequences of the disturbances which are bound to be caused by choosing and implementing one of the organizational alternatives.

All this raises problems of measurement. One can easily advance an objection against the argument of this section by saying that in practice the different outcomes of various action alternatives cannot easily be distinguished unless their probable impact can be measured with a reasonable degree of accuracy. This is admitted. Perhaps the only way to predict the impact is to attempt to measure the degree of acceptability of each alternative on the part of each affected group, or, more precisely, the acceptability of the measures proposed to deal with the issues raised for each group by each alternative. Therefore, if measurement is to be done, the things to be measured have to be defined, and this means that each alternative must be worked out in detail and steps specified by which they are to be implemented. Let us take an example. It is proposed that a new machine should be manned by five men. The process which is being replaced has twenty men working in groups of five. In the existing groups of five there is a hierarchy of skill and differential earnings. The alternative proposed is that the new team of five should comprise men of equal skill. The design of the new machine makes this possible and it seems desirable. If this alternative is adopted, fifteen men will have to be found new jobs or laid off. The decision will have to be made before this alternative is chosen rather than another. What principle is to be adopted to choose the five men from the twenty? The best of the four teams? The youngest five men? The best men from each team plus one other? Fire the lot and get a new team who can freshly learn the new process? Or what? And what wage is to be paid for the new job? Will the wage be half-way between that of a top and bottom crewman on the present process? How acceptable are these detailed plans likely to be to the people affected? Will they resent any attempt at planned redeployment? Or to abolish the differential? Will this raise issues of principle with the trade unions? If these detailed questions were asked about each issue arising for each group, and the results plotted on a scale, the lowest point of which indicates that the group is probably going to resist the proposed change entirely, and the highest that it will find the change quite acceptable, then there is a measure which will discriminate. If there is time available and resources, detailed investigation and fine discrimination might be possible. If there is not enough time, a bigger risk is being taken, but in a real sense it will be a 'calculated' risk.

It is entirely possible and likely that the most acceptable alternative on social grounds gives poor predicted results by technological and economic criteria. If one chooses an alternative which gives a better balanced result, the extent of the social problems to be faced will be clearly revealed. It can now be asked whether the existing mechanisms for redress of grievance are adequate and what else if anything needs to be done. Finally, it remains to assess the economic cost of adopting or not adopting the alternative which promises to maximize economic gain.

Enough has been said to show that the so-called intangibles and immeasurables can be identified, specified and roughly quantified, and that social and psychological problems can be intelligently anticipated if the analysis is carefully done.

While not attempting to sum up this section, perhaps we can, however, attempt some general injunctions to managers whose firms are undergoing change:

1. Set up systematically and in detail the organizational alternatives open.
2. Map out the present organization as a social system, not forgetting its external links.
3. List the groups affected by each organization alternative.
4. Examine the issues likely to be raised in each group from the adoption of each alternative.
5. Assess likely reactions on each issue and 'score' for acceptability.
6. Test economic feasibility against social acceptability and adopt the course which offers the most adaptive and least costly balance.
7. Examine the problems this course raises and ask whether existing means of redress of grievance are adequate to cope. If not, take appropriate steps to create such machinery as seems to be required.

If these seven steps are followed there will be fewer unexpected consequences, always assuming that at some point the people who are to be affected get into the discussion; probably from stage 4 or 5 on. One hopes that this will be seen as being in a real sense 'intelligent anticipation'. It is probably no more than the manager with experience, personal flair and a nose for the systematic in social relations would do anyway. Lesser folk might appreciate the aid that social science offers.

IV

Organization Theory

Organization Theory

So far, we have emphasized in our discussion the relationships between individuals and groups in organizations. Where we have touched upon the relationship between the organization and its wider environment it has been to illuminate the internal problems we were analysing.

We have referred to three distinct but overlapping approaches to these internal problems and have noted their significance for the practice of management. The sociologists, whose work was illustrated by reference mainly to Gouldner and to Weber, concentrate on the factors which shape the structure of organizations and the roles which are played out within them, such as the division of labour and the administrative procedures for authority and control. The industrial psychologists and the 'human relations' school concern themselves chiefly with the problems of the individual, in his efforts to adapt to the physical environment and to technical, administrative and social pulls and pressures; by experiment and observation they have sought for ways to equate efficiency with human satisfaction. The theorists of formal organization, such as Fayol and Urwick, try to derive from the experience of managers some principles of practical use to those who have to design and to maintain organizations.

The critical reader will have noticed at least two shortcomings in the presentation. The first of these is the absence of a common framework to encompass the three approaches. The second is the marked lack of emphasis on an important social process in organizations, that of deciding what is to be done about prices, output, costs and budgets.

There are two chief reasons for the absence so far of much reference to economic decision-making. In the first place, sociologists and psychologists have interested themselves in what happens *after* these matters have been decided. They have tried to explain the social and psychological obstacles to getting things done and in some cases how to overcome them. How what is to be done is decided, has not interested them greatly. As a sociologist, I have naturally placed the emphasis where sociologists usually place it. Secondly, and more importantly perhaps, economists traditionally have not shown much interest in what goes on inside firms, so there was no authoritative view to interpret and discuss in relation to economic decisions. As for the common analytical framework to encompass the sociological and psychological work, this hardly exists. Inevitably, my own attempts to do some integrating have been partial and unsystematic.

It is the purpose of this final section to show that some social scientists have become aware of the need to build a theory of organizations which takes account of the influence of the internal structure on the processes of economic decision-making and the reciprocal effects of economic decisions on internal structures and relationships. To undertake an exhaustive review of this work would need another essay. I propose, therefore, only to exemplify the general direction in which research and theorizing about organization is moving, by reference to recent work by Simon, March and Cyert of the Carnegie Institute of Technology at Pittsburgh, and by Rice of the Tavistock Institute in Britain.

As Cyert and March point out, the economists' theory of the firm is 'primarily a theory of markets . . . [it] purports to explain at a general level the way resources are allocated by a price system'. [38] The theory, they say, was never intended to answer questions about how resources are allocated *within* the firm, nor to explain the social processes by which decisions about prices, outputs and marketing policies are made. They themselves have attempted a theory which answers these questions. They draw heavily on some of the sociological theories of organization to which we have already referred, and to earlier work by March and Simon on more general processes of decision-making in organizations. The theory, it should be added, owes much to investigations of actual processes of decision making.

To the practising manager, the idea that decisions made in organizations about prices and output and budgets are partly the outcome of the problems posed by the economic environment, partly the result of the way various groups and individuals interpret these problems and attempt to influence the processes of decision-taking, will not appear to be novel. Cyert and March have merely taken the idea and have tried to spell out the influences which play upon those who are interpreting the problems posed by the environment and the processes which lead to decisions being taken to deal with them.

A common idea of organization amongst managers, which is partly due to economic theory and partly due to the theory of formal organization, describes organization in terms of activities rationally assigned and co-ordinated to make possible the achievement of an economic objective which is itself a rational response to market forces. Cyert and March prefer the sociologists' model, in which the division of labour required by technology and the scale of operations gives rise to sub-units specialized by task and function, in which the power to influence events is differentially distributed. In this model there is no single rational economic objective; the system of administrative control is not unitary. The organization might well have a number of general goals which might not be consistent with one another. There will be a tendency for sub-units to develop their own goals, which again may be inconsistent with one another and with the organizational goals. On this view, in order to predict what decisions will be made about economic quantities, one would need to know not just that there are economic pressures from the environment. One would ask also: Which information about what parts of the environment reaches what parts of the organization? How does this information affect the aspirations, expectations and goals of the sub-units and how does this in turn influence the 'political' process of deciding what to do? It is not difficult to see the practical potentialities of this sort of theorizing. It encourages straight thinking about the way organizations work and is obviously leading towards a more comprehensive view of their structure and functioning. Surely, if the manager, as a result of his knowledge of such a comprehensive theory comes to know more about what we may describe as the anatomy and physiology of organization, then he will move more intelligently and confidently in his job. Let us look briefly at the outlines of Cyert and March's theory to see whether these remarks seem to be justified.

What do we need to know if we wish to predict which goals (policies) an organization will decide to pursue in relation, for example, to market shares, output levels and product pricing? We should clearly want to investigate the structure to see which sub-units are involved in what Cyert and March refer to as the 'coalition' which decides these things and what their own interests and aims are. We should want to examine the customary processes of bargaining, 'politicking' and rational problem-solving which characterize the 'coalition'. In addition, the structure of power and influence in relation to particular goals and policies would be of concern to us. It would not be enough to say that the organization has certain kinds of problems posed by its environment. We should rather ask what it is about the situation facing the organization which is seen to be problematical, by whom, and why. Pushing further, we would inquire about the way information is sought and given about what goes on inside and outside the organization and how the expectations of groups and sub-units are affected. Knowing what we do about organizations, we should also expect that there would be established routines for solving some kinds of recurring problems and for regulating the flow of information, and we should want to know what these were.

But a theory has to be more than just a check-list of questions and categorizing of questions. There must be some way of describing analytically the relations between the factors covered in the questioning. All our questions so far (which are only a small part of the range discussed by Cyert and March) have assumed that there is going to be conflict and uncertainty in the decision-making process. The organization implied in these questions is ridden with risk and uncertainty and is conflict-generating. One has to agree, I am sure, that organizations *have* problems of resolving internal conflict and of coping with the uncertainties of markets, supplies and governments policies. These could be described as centrifugal tendencies. Yet it is also an observed fact that organizations cohere and survive. So there must be centripetal tendencies at work too. Cyert and March argue, from the empirical evidence, that conflict is always latent in organizations. Whether it remains so depends upon the operation of certain social and administrative mechanisms. Amongst these are the delegation of problem-solving, which means that sub-units and individuals solve limited, defined problems, in what they see as rational ways. Any inconsistency with others' solutions to other limited problems is not clearly perceived. Decentralization of the authority to make the rules governing decision-taking is also conflict-avoiding, provided that the rules are generally acceptable. Finally, the organization tends to take in sequence and not in parallel the consideration of goals or policies which are likely to conflict.

As to uncertainty, the further one peers into the future the more vague and uncertain that future becomes. This applies to organizations as well as to individuals. Therefore, organizations tend to the kind of forward planning which eschews long-term prediction and promises short-term control. This means that organizations usually attend to pressing problems as they arise and at the same time try to structure the environment (e.g. by pacts with competitors and suppliers) to minimize long-term uncertainty.

The empirical evidence suggests to Cyert and March that organizations rarely look at the complexities of their environment with a view to understanding them. Nor do they merely pick up random information. The information-gathering process seems to start with the appearance of what is conceived by the organization, or by part of it, as a problem. Then the simplest possible explanation of why the problem has arisen is proposed and this forms the basis of information-seeking and decision-making, until it is shown that something more complicated is needed as a matter of practical necessity. It seems to Cyert and March as if this process of economy in explanation, added to the previously mentioned 'breaking down' of complex problems into simple ones, and the acceptance of decision rules, ensures some consistency of goals and helps to keep down the amount of conflict and uncertainty.

Obviously Cyert and March are attracted by the resemblance of an organization to a living organism, with its power to adapt to a changing environment through its reactions to the stresses and strains generated by conflict and uncertainty. It is claimed, persuasively, that organizations, like individuals, have the power to learn from experience how to survive. They learn how to change their goals, how to revise procedures and rules, how to look for and to find new and significant information. To be sure, they do this through the agency of people, but, as we have seen, individuals are under strong influence to behave according to the roles defined for them.

Working largely independently, research workers at the Tavistock Institute have gone further than most in building a framework which can bind together the various psychological and sociological theories of organizations. In his book *The Enterprise and its Environment*[39] A. K. Rice, a member of the Tavistock group, elaborates a conceptual framework which, as he says:

'relates individuals, groups, and institutions to each other in one coherent system.'

What follows is a free summary of Rice's account.

The framework proposed by Rice exhibits the organization as a series of 'encapsulated significant environments'.* The individual member of

*My term—T.L.

an organization has his internal world and an external world, which importantly includes the other individuals with whom he constantly interacts on the job. This working group is a significant environment for the individual, in which he seeks satisfactory relationships. The group too has its own internal life, which comprises the complex of interpersonal relations, influenced by shared or discrepant norms of behaviour, common or conflicting beliefs and attitudes. It has its own external environment composed of adjacent groups and individuals. A sub-unit of a large organization might include many such groups, and its internal system is described by the relationships between them. Its environment consists of other sub-units and the organization as a whole. The organization, i.e. the whole complex of interrelated and encapsulated sub-units, groups, and individuals, has to adapt to a changing world which includes other groups and organizations such as shareholders, customers, trades unions and governments.

The internal life of an organization is characterized by transactions across the boundaries of groups and sub-groups by individuals who manage the relationships between the groups and their several environments. As we know from our previous analysis, the division of labour which is created to achieve what Rice calls the 'primary task'* of the organization, helps shape the structure of sub-units and groupings and allocates to them their specific primary task. We have also had occasion to note that the effective pursuit by one group of its task might bring it into conflict with another.† We also know that the interrelations between individuals, groups and sub-units give rise to customary ways of doing things which are not officially prescribed and to equally unofficial transactions, all in the process of adjusting and adapting to the demands of the environment.

To Rice, as to the economist, an organization is an 'open system'. It takes in inputs from the environment, converts them, and sends outputs back into the environment. His 'operating systems', i.e. the sub-units to which we have referred, either deal with inputs or outputs, or carry out processes of conversion. Of course each operating system has its own input–conversion–output procedure. The management of the organization is made up of those *general managers* who stand at the 'boundary' of the whole system and its environment, the *operating managers* who stand at the boundary of the operating systems, and the *managers of the*

*i.e. the task which has to be performed if the organization is to survive.
†For example, in Gouldner's study of succession.

control and service functions who stand inside the boundary and whose job it is to integrate the various operating systems so that they serve the 'overall primary task' of the organization.

The concept of *system*, crucial to this theory of organization, has not yet been defined. *System* expresses the idea of a set of parts related to each other in patterns (or configurations) which mark them off from other systems with different patterns. The idea of a system also entails the idea of a boundary, an environment and equilibrating mechanisms. These mechanisms are set in motion when changes take place in the environment which affect one or other parts of the system and which induce stresses which must be relieved by a re-ordering of the parts. We have described an organization as a series of systems within systems. We now add the concept of mechanisms of adjustment and realignment which will be set in motion by changes in the environment.

The organization, with its sub-systems, groups and individuals, does not react automatically in its environment. The processes through which equilibrium is sought result from conscious decisions and activities of individuals and groups. Someone has to decide what changes have to be made in response to environmental stimuli, whether to diversify products, to purchase a new machine, to employ a personnel manager. Someone has to define new tasks and create new organizational configurations. On these decisions will partly depend the successful adaptation of the system. But not wholly. The organizational strategy might run counter to the smooth adaptation of a sub-group to *its* environment and then there will be resistance to change. Or the strategic decision itself might be ill-suited to the wider environment, because of pressures from inside the system. It is because organizations do not have built-in automatic mechanisms of adaptation such as animals have, nor mechanical systems of feed-back and control such as an engine governor has,* that the practice of management is of such great importance, and so are the administrative procedures which provide information and 'cues' to set in motion processes of adaptation. This is why new sciences like cybernetics are important to management, because in one aspect an organization is a system of information flows. Computers are also invaluable as part of a more efficient system of information feedback. But, as March and Simon point out, even

---

*Although some administration procedures incorporate quasi-mechanical feedback; the stock-control system mentioned earlier is one example.

with all these aids the 'central nervous system' of a human organization is still an extremely crude mechanism.

Such 'models' as those we have been discussing, of the structure and functioning of organizations, need to be simple enough in their construction to be of use in analysis and complicated enough to be realistic. To the social scientist they are attractive because they explain things that were not adequately explained before; they suggest hypotheses for research, the results of which ought, by confirmation or modification, to enhance their value. Managers will, I hope, be persuaded by this brief account to study them and to employ them as aids to the definition and diagnosis of their problems.

Conclusion

We live in a world of rapid technical change and of complex large-scale organization. To understand organizations and their problems of change is very difficult while the traditional frontiers between the social sciences remain inviolate and while the gap between the social and natural sciences is so wide. Happily, the frontiers seem to be opening up rapidly and the gaps are closing. The similarities between the work of Rice, of March, Simon and Cyert, and of a political scientist like William J. Gore[40] show this and suggest the possibility of a new discipline of organization study.

Recently social scientists from many disciplines came together to discuss their problems in studying organizations and published their deliberations.[41] All the signs are that before very long we shall have an accepted theory of organization. As we have seen, there have been many approaches, but nobody seems quite to have arrived yet. Yet already the practical value of what has been done is being demonstrated. Social scientific 'models' of organization are being fed into computers, so that the effects of changes in certain variables can be studied for their effects on other parts of the system and for their outcome in terms of profitability and efficiency. All this, as it develops, will add up to considerable practical help to those who have the responsibility for managing organizations. If this essay has succeeded in persuading a few managers of this, then it will have been worth while.

References

1. BARNARD, C. 'Education for Executives.' *The Journal of Business*, 1945, Vol. 18, p. 175.
2. GLUCKMAN, MAX (Ed.). *Closed Systems and Open Minds*. London: Oliver and Boyd, 1964, p. 160.
3. TAYLOR, F. W. *Scientific Management*. New York: Harper and Brothers, 1947.
4. WEBER, MAX. *From Max Weber: Essays in Sociology*. Trans. Gerth and Mills. Oxford, 1946.
5. MYERS, C. S. *Industrial Psychology in Great Britain*. London: Jonathan Cape, 1933.
6. ROETHLISBERGER, F. J. and DICKSON, W. J. *Management and the Worker*. Cambridge, Mass.: Harvard U.P., 1939, p. 86.
7. ROETHLISBERGER, F. J. and DICKSON, W. J. Op. cit., p. 160.
8. ROETHLISBERGER, F. J. and DICKSON, W. J. Op. cit., p. 185.
9. URWICK, L. *The Elements of Administration*. New York: Harper and Brothers, 1943.
10. FAYOL, H. *General and Industrial Administration*. London: Pitman, 1949.
11. BURNS, TOM and STALKER, G. M. *The Management of Innovation*. Tavistock, 1961.
12. WOODWARD, JOAN. *Management and Technology*. London: H.M.S.O., 1959.
13. SCOTT, W. H., BANKS, J., HALSEY, A. H. and LUPTON, T. *Technical Change and Industrial Relations*. Liverpool University Press, 1956.
14. WALKER, C. R. and GUEST, R. H. *The Man on the Assembly Line*. Cambridge, Mass: Harvard U.P., 1952.
15. ROY, D. 'Efficiency and the Fix.' *Amer. J. Sociol.*, Vol. LX, No. 3, Nov. 1954.
16. LUPTON, T. *On the Shop Floor*. Oxford: Pergamon Press, 1963.
17. CUNNISON, SHEILA. *Wages and Work Allocation*. London: Tavistock, 1965.
18. SAYLES, L. *Behaviour in Industrial Work Groups*. New York: Wiley, 1958.
19. LEWIN, K. *Field Theory in Social Science*. London: Tavistock, 1951.
20. HOMANS, G. C. *The Human Group*, London. Routledge & Kegan Paul, 1951.
21. ZALEZNIK, A., CHRISTENSEN, C. R. and ROETHLISBERGER, F. J. *The Motivation, Productivity and Satisfaction of Workers: A Predictive Study*. Boston: Harvard Graduate School of Business Administration, 1958.
22. MERTON, R. K. *Social Theory and Social Structure*. Glencoe, Ill.: The Free Press, 1957.
23. PUGH, D. S. *et al*. 'A Conceptual Scheme for Organisational Analysis.' *Administrative Science Quarterly*, Vol. 8, No. 3, Dec. 1963.
24. GOULDNER, A. W. *Patterns of Industrial Bureaucracy*. London: Routledge and Kegan Paul, 1955.
25. GOULDNER, A. W. *Wildcat Strike*. London: Routledge and Kegan Paul, 1955.
26. FRIEDMANN, G. *Industrial Society*. Glencoe, Ill.: The Free Press, 1955.
27. WOODWARD, JOAN. Op. cit., p. 4.

28. TRIST, E. L., HIGGIN, G. W., MURRAY, H. and POLLOCK, A. B. *Organizational Choice*. London: Tavistock, 1963.

29. FLANDERS, A. *The Fawley Productivity Agreements*. London: Faber and Faber, 1964.

30. GRAY, A. P. and ABRAMS, M. *Construction of Esso Refinery, Fawley: a Study in Organization*. London: British Institute of Management, 1954.

31. DUBIN, R. *Human Relations in Administration*. Englewood Cliffs, N.J.: Prentice-Hall, 1962. (This is a collection of the best readings in the social science of management, with a linking commentary of great value.)

32. JAQUES, E. *The Changing Culture of a Factory*. London: Tavistock, 1951.

33. JAQUES, E. *Measurement of Responsibility*. London: Tavistock, 1956.

34. BROWN, W. *Exploration in Management*. London: Heinemann, 1960.

35. LIKERT, R. *New Patterns of Management*. New York: McGraw-Hill, 1961.

36. MCGREGOR, D. *Human Side of Enterprise*. New York: McGraw-Hill, 1960.

37. ARGYRIS, C. *Personality and Organization*. New York: Harper and Brothers, 1957.

38. CYERT, R. M. and MARCH, J. G. *A Behavioral Theory of the Firm*. Englewood Cliffs, N.J.: Prentice-Hall, 1963.

39. RICE, A. K. *The Enterprise and its Environment*. London: Tavistock, 1963.

40. GORE, W. J. *Administrative Decision Making*. New York: Wiley, 1964.

41. LEAVITT, H. J. (Ed.). *The Social Science of Organizations*. Englewood Cliffs, N.J.: Prentice-Hall, 1963. (A selection of interesting papers from an interdisciplinary seminar in the U.S.A.)

A Note on Further Reading

In addition to the works expressly mentioned in the text and listed above, I have used the following works:

FOGARTY, M. P. *The Rules of Work*. London: Geoffrey Chapman, 1963.

GLUCKMAN, MAX. *Custom and Conflict in Africa*. Oxford: Blackwell, 1956.

LEAVITT, H. J. *Managerial Psychology*. Chicago, U.P., Phoenix Books, 1956 (Paperback). (An elementary introduction to some findings of social science which are relevant to management. It is clearly and wittily written.)

LITTERER, J. A. *Organizations: Structure and Behaviour*. New York: Wiley and Sons, 1953. (Another collection of articles and selections from books, with a linking commentary.)

LUPTON, T. *Money for Effort*. London: H.M.S.O., 1960.

LUPTON, T. *Industrial Behaviour and Personnel Management*. London: Institute of Personnel Management, 1964.

MASSIE, J. L. *Essentials of Management*. Englewood Cliffs, N.J.: Prentice-Hall, 1964. (This paperback describes mathematical techniques in a treatment suitable for the 'lay' manager, and gives references to more specialized books in the same field.)

The manager who wishes to follow the discussion on the issues raised in this essay would be advised to start with this general list of books together with Brown (34), Dubin (31) and Leavitt (41), and then to move from them to more detailed field researches.

Index of Names

Index